Favell Lee Mortimer

Streaks of light

Fifty-two facts from the Bible for the fifty-two Sundays of the year

Favell Lee Mortimer

Streaks of light
Fifty-two facts from the Bible for the fifty-two Sundays of the year

ISBN/EAN: 9783337270384

Printed in Europe, USA, Canada, Australia, Japan

Cover: Foto ©Andreas Hilbeck / pixelio.de

More available books at **www.hansebooks.com**

STREAKS OF LIGHT

OR

FIFTY-TWO FACTS FROM THE BIBLE

FOR THE

Fifty-two Sundays of the Year

BY THE AUTHOR OF 'PEEP OF DAY,' &c.

The Lord of all a babe became,
  A babe like others seen,
As small in size and weak of frame
  As babes have always been.'

HART.

Seventy-first Thousand

LONDON
HATCHARDS, PICCADILLY
1890

PREFACE.

THIS little work appeared before under the title of *Tracts for Children in Streets and Lanes, Highways and Hedges.*

While it bore this humble title, it wore a humble dress. Now having assumed a more elegant one, it aspires to a higher title : thus reversing the usual order of things, in which the dress is made to suit the title ; whereas in this case the title is made to suit the dress.

But though it may, by means of its better dress and better title, gain admittance into better places than highways and hedges, still its office is as humble as before : and that office is to teach the children of the POOR. It is an offering made to the Ragged-School Teacher, the Sunday-School Teacher, and the District Visitor.

Each lesson can be understood by those who have no previous knowledge ; and each is calculated to be the *first* address to one who has never before heard of God or His Christ ; whether read by a Ragged-School Teacher in an alley, or by a swarthy Catechist under a tree.

If lent to cottagers by District Visitors, this lowly book will be read by some dim eyes which have never conned the second page of a sermon.

But though designed for village school-rooms and lowly dwellings, its voice has reached the nurseries of the RICH. Children in worked frocks and silk sashes have sat on the Saviour's knees, as well as the tattered and bare-footed.

One of those drawing-room pets, though unable to read a single line, carried this book into her nursery. Soon afterwards—the victim of scarlatina—she was removed from the nursery into the highest attic. From her sickbed she sent for her favourite, and turning away her eyes from the gaudy pages of earthly story-books, she fixed them upon Jesus alone, as she listened to the voice of her nurse reading these sacred stories, and the accompanying hymns— (sweet strains played by various hands on the infant lyre.)

The LAST of her forty-five fleeting months was spent in fellowship with Jesus. Her best-loved song began

     ' Here we suffer grief and pain '

and of that song, her best-loved stanza was

> ‘ Oh, how happy we shall be!
> For our Saviour we shall see
> Exalted on His throne.
> Oh, that will be joyful !’

She had also her favourite stories. Among them were ‘ The Happy Night,’ and ‘ The Happy Morning.’

When HER happy morning came—which was the morning of Palm Sunday (the morning on which babes warbled forth their songs of praise in the Saviour’s presence) when that morning came—that long-desired—that ever-to-be-remembered—that dark-bright morning—this lovely, loving infant, lifted up her eyes—her bright—blue —-celestial eyes, and gazing intently upon an unearthly vision—whispered, ‘Pretty Lord !’

It was the language of a BABE ; but it was the sentiment of an APOSTLE. For thus John spake of HIM, ‘ His countenance was as the sun shineth in his strength.’

‘ Pretty ! pretty !’ lisped the babe.

‘ Glorious ! glorious !’ shout all the angels round the throne.

Her EVERLASTING song began when Ada whispered, ‘ Pretty Lord !’ All the songs of heaven are but modulations of the theme, 'Thou art fairer than the children of men!' Ps. xlv, 2.

Fair—exceeding fair didst thou appear to us —sweet infant, in all the flower of thy baby-hood—scarce four years;—but fairer—fairer far did thy Lord appear to thee in all the brightness of His glory at the right hand of God. And fair—divinely fair—wilt thou be—when thou comest with HIM amongst HIS white-robed innocents.

₊ *The Story of Ada, by her Mother*, is still in cir-culation.

CONTENTS.

STREAKS OF LIGHT.

THIS WORLD.

ONCE there was a deaf and dumb boy, who used to wonder how the world was made. At last, he was taught to understand signs with the fingers, and then he was told who made the world. How much delighted he was to find that God made the world!

What is God like? Nothing that you have seen. A picture of Him could not be drawn, because He has not a body like you and me; He is a Spirit. He is everywhere but there is one place in which He lives: it is called heaven. I cannot tell you where it is. No bird could fly to that place; but angels often come down from heaven into this world.

And who are angels? They are spirits.

There are good angels in heaven with God.
They have no bodies. But they are not
everywhere, as God is.

Who made the angels? It was God.
Once God was alone in heaven. But He
did not choose to be always alone. He made
the angels. Some of them grew wicked,
and He turned them out of heaven. Those
wicked angels are called devils.

At last God made this world in which we
live. Of what did He make it? Of nothing.
How did He make it? By speaking,—He
said, ' Let there be light.'

This world is very large. What shape is
it? You have seen the moon—this world is
the same shape as the moon. Do you think
it is flat like a plate, or shilling? Oh, no;
it is round like an orange. Many children
think the world is flat, and then they wonder
what is at the edge of the world. They think
to themselves, ' If I were to travel a great
way, at last I should come to the edge;' but
they never would.

If a fly were walking on an orange,
would it ever come to the edge? No! when

it had gone a great way, it would come round to the same place again where it was at first; and so would you if you were to travel a very long way without ever turning back.

Most of the world is covered over with the great sea, and part of it is dry land.

Once the land was all bare, but God spake, and it was covered with grass, and flowers, and trees, and corn.

Once it was empty. No one lived in it; but God spake, and fishes swam in the waters, and birds flew in the air, and reptiles crept upon the ground, and beasts walked there.

But not one of all these creatures could understand. Then God made a man. He took the dust of the ground, and made a body for the man, and then He breathed into him, and He gave him a soul. The man could understand and think of God. His name was called Adam. God took a piece of his flesh and bone and made a woman, and she, too, could think of God.

Can you, my dear child, think of God?

I am sure you can. You listen now that I am telling you about Him. If I were to talk to a little dog, or to a cow, or to a sheep about God, would it listen? Oh, no. What is the reason of this? The dog has a body, but it has no spirit. You, my child, have a spirit. God gave you a spirit or soul, as well as a body.

I once heard of a little child of two years old, who said to her mother, 'Who made me? some one must have made me.' Her mother said, 'It was God, my child. He made you: He takes care of you, He gives you food and clothes, and all you have—He is very, very kind to you.'

'*Then*,' said the little darling, looking up quite pleased in her mother's face,—'*then* I love Him.'

This little child loved God still more, when she heard how kind God has been in sending His own dear Son from heaven to die for us. This is the kindest of all the kind things that God has done.

Whenever you like, you may speak to God. He is always near, and can hear you.

I know you have done many naughty things, but God is willing to forgive you.

Here is a little prayer just fit for you: 'O Heavenly Father, forgive me for the sake of Thy dear Son Jesus Christ.'

'God made all the things I see,
  And beautiful they are;
But things I have not seen there are,
  More sweet and beauteous far.

God has made a glorious place,
  A golden land of light,
Where holy children see His face,
  And walk with Him in white.'

Songs of Praise by Mrs. Bevan.

II

THE OLD SERPENT; OR, ADAM AND EVE.

WHEN children are very little, they begin to do wrong. A child will sometimes, when its mother is not looking, slily take a pinch of sugar out of the basin, or when its mother is out of the room it will go to the cupboard and help itself to sugar, fruit, or nice red jam. Is it not very naughty of little children ever to behave in this way? But this is not all. When a little child is caught in doing wrong, it will often deny it. If the mother finds it at the cupboard, it will say it has not taken anything—when it has. It would be well if children were ashamed of their naughtiness, but they will sometimes laugh about it. I have seen children look at each other and laugh about what they had done wrong. But God is angry at sin.

Is it *children* only who are wicked? Do not men and women do many wrong things?

Yes; there are men and women who swear, who steal, who call names, and say what is not true.

How is it people are so wicked? Did God make them wicked? Oh, no! God is good; He never made anybody wicked. It is the devil who makes people wicked. I will tell you how he made the first man and woman wicked.

Their names were Adam and Eve. God made their bodies out of the dust of the ground. He gave them souls as well as bodies; and they could think of Him, and understand what He said. Beasts and birds have no souls: they cannot think of God. Adam and Eve were very good. They loved each other, and they loved God better still. They were very happy. They lived in a sweet Garden, called the Garden of Eden,— or Paradise. You never saw such a garden as that.

It was full of fruit-trees. God allowed Adam and Eve to eat the fruit. But He told them not to eat of the fruit of one tree which grew in the middle of the garden.

He said, 'If you eat of the fruit of that tree, you shall die.'

The devil did not like to see Adam and Eve so happy. He is very miserable himself, and he wishes everybody to be miserable. Once he was a good angel, and lived with God; but he grew wicked, and was cast down to hell. The devil came into the Garden of Eden. He is called the Old Serpent, because he is so sly. He said to Eve, 'Has God said that you may not eat of every tree in the garden?'

And Eve said, 'We may eat of the fruit of all the trees, except of one. God has said, if we eat that, or even touch it, we shall die.'

Then the serpent said, 'You shall not die, but if you eat of that fruit you shall become wise like God.'

The serpent knew this was not true.

Why did Eve believe him sooner than God?

She took some of the fruit, and she gave some to Adam.

They soon found out how foolish they had

been. They were not happy now; they were sinners; they had disobeyed the commandment of God.

When they heard God speaking in the garden, they were frightened, and hid themselves among the trees. How foolish it was to think they could hide themselves from God! Cannot God, who made the trees, see through the thickest boughs?

God might have left Adam to himself, and let the devil take him away to hell. But God is very good and kind. He spoke to Adam, and said, 'Where art thou?'

Adam was obliged to answer God, but he did not speak as he ought; he said that the woman had *given* him of the fruit,—that was a bad excuse. Why did he *take* the fruit?

Eve said it was the serpent's fault, — that was a bad excuse. Why did she believe the serpent?

God was most angry with the serpent; He cursed him. But He did not curse Adam and Eve.

He told Adam he must work hard to get

his bread, and He told Eve that she would have much trouble with her little children; and He turned them both out of the garden. But God did not curse Adam and Eve; He loved them, and wished to save them from being for ever in hell with the devil.

God has an only Son, whom He loves. He promised to send His only Son to die instead of Adam and Eve, and all their children.

How kind it was of God to send His dear Son to die for *us*, that we might not be cursed for ever!

We are Adam's children, and we should go to hell if it were not for Jesus Christ, the Son of God. We are sinners like Adam and Eve. Why is it that children ever steal and say what is not true? Because they are the children of Adam and Eve, who took the fruit.

Your bodies must turn to dust in the grave,—will your souls go to hell? I hope not. There is One who can save you. Go to Jesus, He is in heaven now, but He can hear you. Say to Him, 'Pardon a sinful child.' Ask Him very often to forgive you. Ask God, His Father, to forgive you for the sake of His dear Son Jesus; and ask for the Holy Spirit to make you good.— Then you will hate lying, and fighting, and calling names.

' When man at first was made by God,
    In glory, glory, glory,
No sin nor sorrow found abode
    In glory, glory, glory.

But soon, alas! our father fell,
    From glory, glory, glory,
And rather chose the way of hell,
    Than glory, glory, glory.

But God beheld our ruin'd race,
    From glory, glory, glory;
And Jesus left His happy place,
    In glory, glory, glory.

He died on the accursed tree,
    Sing glory, glory, glory;
To bring poor sinners, such as we,
    To glory, glory, glory.'

III.

THE FIRST MURDER; OR, CAIN AND ABEL.

HAVE you ever heard an account of a murder? I know you have. Men often go about the streets singing a song about a murder, and selling a paper about it.

Who was the man that dared to commit the first murder? His name was Cain; his father and mother were called Adam and Eve, and they were the first man and woman whom God made. Cain was their first baby. His mother was pleased when she saw her baby, for she did not know what a wicked man he would grow up.

Eve had another son, whom she called Abel. He grew up to be a good man. God gave Abel His Holy Spirit to make him good, and Abel loved God, and tried to please Him.

Cain soon found out that God loved Abel better than himself, and this made him angry. Why did not Cain ask God to give him His Holy Spirit, too? Then he would have been good, like Abel.

I daresay you have sometimes seen a naughty, sulky child sitting in a corner of the room, not choosing to speak to anybody, or, if he spoke, grumbling and calling names. That naughty child was like Cain.

God in the sky sees all the people in this world. He sees the wicked thoughts in their hearts, as well as their wicked looks.

This great God spoke to wicked Cain, and said, 'Why are you angry? Why do you look displeased?'

It was very kind of the great God to speak to this sinful man; but Cain would not mind—he went on in his wickedness.

One day he was with Abel all alone, when a dreadful thing happened.

While they were talking, Cain rose up against Abel and killed him. I do not know how he killed him, whether with a stone or a great stick, but that is no matter,—poor Abel lay bleeding on the earth,—the blood ran into the ground. Oh, it must have been a dreadful sight! How did Cain feel when he saw his brother's blood, and that good brother cold, and pale, and still, like a stone?

Cain thought he could hide his sin from every eye, because he was alone when he did it. But he forgot that God saw him.

Soon God spoke to him. He said, 'Where is Abel, thy brother?'

Cain answered, 'I do not know. Am I my brother's keeper?'

You see he dared to tell God a lie.

Then God told him that he should not stay in that place. Cain was not to live any more with his father and mother, and his brothers and sisters, and their children. He was to go to some place far off, where he would hear of God no more.

He did not like this; for, though he did not love God, he was afraid of being sent far away; he thought, also, that anybody who found him would kill him.

But God set a mark upon him, to show people that Cain was not to be killed.

So Cain went a great way off, and he had a wife and children ; and he built a city for his grandchildren and great-grandchildren. But was he happy ? Wicked people cannot be happy. God let him live and gave him children, but God did not love him.

What becomes of liars when they die, and what becomes of murderers ? They will go to hell ! That is a horrible, dark, and burning place, far off from God. The devil is the father of liars and murderers, and he wishes to have them in his own place.

Abel did not go to hell when he died ; his body lay bleeding on the earth, but his soul went up to God in heaven. There he saw his Saviour, the Son of God, who had promised to die for his sins.

Abel has been singing in heaven a long while. He was the *first* who began to praise God for pardoning his sins, and now there are hundreds and thousands joining in his songs.

I hope the child who reads this book will one day be praising God in heaven with Abel. and will say, 'Praise Him who loved us, and washed us from our sins in His own blood.'

If you want to go to that happy place, go and pray to God alone, and say, ' O great God, pardon all the naughty things I have done, and make me good by the Holy Spirit, because Thy dear Son died upon the cross for me.'

> ' There is beyond the sky
>   A heaven of joy and love,
> And holy children, when they die,
>   Go to that world above.
>
> There is a dreadful hell,
>   And everlasting pains ;
> There sinners must with devils dwell,
>   In darkness, fire, and chains
>
> WATTS.

IV.

THE GREAT RAIN.

ONCE the whole world was drowned. Yes, all the people in the world were drowned, and all the beasts **and** birds except one family, and a few beasts and **birds** with them. How did this happen? Did **you** ever hear about it?

It happened four thousand years ago.

This world was full of people then, **as it** is now, and it was full of wicked people. The great God who made the world cannot bear wickedness; He looked down and saw the people fighting, and stealing, and killing each other. At last He said He would drown them all, **except** one good man, and his wife, **and** his children. The name of this man was Noah.

God told Noah **to** build a great place called an ark. It was to be built so that it could float on **the** water like a ship, only it was not to have a mast **or** sails like a ship.

The ark was to be made of wood, and covered with pitch, and lined with pitch, to keep out the wet. There were to be three great rooms in the ark, one above the other, and there was to be a window at the top, and a door at the side. God told Noah to take some of all sorts of beasts and birds into the ark with him; but first he was to get food for them, such as hay for the horses, and seed for the birds.

When the ark was finished, God told Noah to go in, and to take the beasts and birds in with him. What a strange sight it must have been to see the beasts and birds going into the ark! If God had not made them quiet and obedient, Noah never could have brought them in.

Noah had three sons, and they had three wives, so that there were eight people who went into the ark.

None of the wicked people went in.

Noah had often begged them to repent and to turn to God, but they had not minded. They would not believe that they should at last be drowned.

As soon as Noah was in the ark, God Himself shut the door.

No one could get into the ark after God had shut the door.

That day the rain began to pour down from the sky, and the water came up out of the ground. All that day it rained, and the next, and the next, and for nearly six weeks. Such rain was never seen before, nor ever will be seen again. Everybody was drowned, and every beast and every bird. If people climbed to the tops of the trees, the water soon reached them; and if they mounted the high hills, the waters at last covered them; there was no way of escaping from the anger of God. Once God would have heard the prayers of these sinners, but now it was too late—they were all drowned.

For nearly a year Noah floated in his ark upon the waters.

Once he sent out a raven to see whether the land was dry, but the bird never came back.

Another time he sent out a dove, and this

sweet bird came to the window again, and
Noah put out his hand, and pulled her in.
The poor little dove had found no bough on
which to rest, and she liked to return to
the ark, while the raven chose to fly about
till the earth was dry.

Noah waited one week, and then he sent
out the dove again, and this time she returned with the branch of an olive-tree in
her beak; then Noah knew that the tops of
the trees were seen.

In another week he sent out his good
little dove again, and this time she came
back no more.

Still Noah would not leave the ark till
God told him.

At last God said to him, 'Go out of the
ark with your wife, and your sons, and
your sons' wives, and the beasts, and the
birds, and the creeping things.' Then they
all went out.

How glad must the stag have been to
bound once more in the forests! How glad
must the eagle have been to soar once more
in the air! And how sweetly the lark

must have sung, as it flew out of the window, and saw again the bright sun!

But were beasts and birds as glad as Noah? Oh, no; he knew who had saved him from dying in the waters. He loved God for His goodness, and praised Him, and prayed to Him.

God promised He would never again drown the world, and He gave a sign that He would remember His promise; that sign you have seen,—it is the beautiful rainbow which shines in the sky when the sun is beginning to shine, and the showers are almost over. That rainbow puts us in mind of God's kindness to Noah.

But though the world will never be drowned again, something else still more dreadful will happen. It will be burned up! Who will be saved in that day?

Only those who have believed in Jesus Christ. He died for our sins, that we might be saved from eternal fire.

See Gen. vi, vii, viii, and ix, 1–17; 2 Peter, last chapter.

'There was a noble ark,
  Sailing o'er waters dark,
    And wide around;
  Not one tall tree was seen,
  Nor flower, nor leaf of green,
    All—all were drowned.

Then a soft wing was spread,
And o'er the billows dread
  A meek dove flew;
But on that shoreless tide
No living thing she spied
  To cheer her view.

So to the ark she fled,
With weary, drooping wing.
  To seek for rest:
Christ is thine ark, my love;
Thou art the tender dove;
  Fly to His breast.'

MRS. SIGOURNEY.

V.

THE FIRE ON THE MOUNTAIN.

Do you think any one ever heard God speak? Should you be frightened if God were to speak from heaven? Yes, I know you would.

Once God spoke to a great many people; He spoke in a very loud voice, so that they could all hear.

Who were these people? They were called the people of Israel: they did not live in a town like London: they were amongst the hills; at night they slept in their tents. They were going to a country a great way off, and they moved their tents from place to place.

There was a good man who took care of them, called Moses.

God was their King.

One day God spoke to the people of Israel. In the morning there was a noise of thunder and the sound of a trumpet, very loud indeed.

The people heard the noise in their tents, and they trembled

Moses told the people to come out of their tents to see God; and so all the people stood round about the mountain.

What a sight they beheld! The Lord was come down in fire, and there was a great deal of smoke, and the mountain shook. There was a dreadful sound as well. The noise of the trumpet grew louder and louder.

At last God spoke. What did He say? He gave the people ten laws. They are called the Ten Commandments.

While God was speaking, the mountain went on smoking, and the people were so frightened that they went further off, for they were afraid of being killed. They said to Moses, 'Do *you* speak to us, and we will hear; let not God speak to us or we shall die.' So, after that, God did not speak to the people, but He told Moses what to say.

Moses went up quite near to God, and listened to His words. The people of Israel saw him go up the mountain, till he was hid by the great cloud of smoke.

When Moses came down from the mountain he brought in his arms two great pieces of stone, on which God had written the ten laws.

The next time you go to church you might see the ten commandments, for they are copied out, and written up at one end of the church.

I have **heard of a thief who** once went into a church,—not to pray,—but to steal. He meant to put his hand into people's pockets, and take away their handkerchiefs and their money. But before he began to steal, he looked up and saw the ten laws. One of them is,

' Thou shalt not steal.

The thief had never heard this law before. He felt frightened, and he did not dare to put his hand into anybody's pocket. He went home, repented of his sins, and believed in Jesus.

You have done a great many naughty things. God could punish you.

The Son of God minded all the ten laws, yet He was punished.

Why was the Son of God punished?

That you might be forgiven. Ask God to forgive you for the sake of Jesus. Say to God,—'I have not obeyed Thy laws: I am a sinner. But Jesus was punished instead of me. Oh, forgive me for His sake!'

You may read about Moses in the Bible, in Exodus xix and xx.

These are the ten commandments:—

I. Thou shalt **have no** other **gods** before Me.

II. Thou shalt not make unto **thee** any **graven** image. Thou shalt not bow down thyself to them, nor serve **them.**

III. Thou shalt not take the name **of the** Lord thy God in **vain.**

IV. Remember the Sabbath-day, to keep it holy.

V. Honour thy father and thy mother.

VI. Thou shalt not kill.

VII. Thou shalt not commit adultery.

VIII. Thou shalt not steal.

IX. Thou shalt not **bear false** witness against thy neighbour.

X. Thou shalt not covet.

VI.

THE RAVENS.

WHILE we are sleeping in our beds there is One above the sky who is making the food to grow out of the earth. He makes the little seed of corn spring up into a tall stalk, and then turn yellow, and bend under the weight of the grain at the top.

When the corn is ripe, the reaper comes and cuts it down and binds it into sheaves and fills the wagon, and lays it by in the barn ; then the thresher beats out the grain from the husks.

Then the corn is put into a sack and carried to the miller to grind into flour; then the flour is put into a sack and carried to the baker, and it is baked in the oven: when it is taken out it is fit to be eaten.

Is it men who make the bread or God ? It is God who makes the corn to grow; if God were not to make the corn, we could have no bread to eat. Sometimes God

will not make the corn grow. Why?
Because men are wicked, and **God** is angry
with them.

The land of Israel is very hot. One year
God sent no rain to make the ground soft,
so the corn did not grow up. The people
in that land were very wicked. They
bowed down to images of wood and stone,
and prayed to them, and said, 'Take care of
us ; you are our gods.'

There was a good man in that land who
loved God. His name was Elijah. When
there was very little bread, God would not
let him starve. He told him to go and live
by the side of a certain brook or pond, and
He said, ' I have desired the ravens to feed
ou there.' What ! birds to feed a man ?
I have often heard of a man feeding birds,
but I never heard before of birds feeding a
man,—and such birds too, as ravens ! not
gentle birds, but fierce creatures, ready to
pick out your eyes with their great beaks :
but God can make fierce ravens gentle as
doves, if He please.

Elijah believed what God said, and he

D

went to live by the side of a brook or pond, among the trees. I do not think he had any house there, but it was so warm that he could sleep out of doors. He was quite alone, yet he could speak to his Friend in heaven; I mean his God.

Did his heavenly Father keep His promise? Oh, yes. In the morning the birds came. I cannot tell how many, but there were more than one. What did they bring with them? Pieces of bread and of meat. I suppose they carried them in their beaks. God had sent His birds to feed His dear son Elijah. The ravens were the servants of Elijah.

In the evening they came again, and brought Elijah his supper.

Every morning and every evening they came; they never missed. His Father in heaven never forgot to feed Elijah. He gave him two meals every day, breakfast and supper. Most people have dinner as well, but Elijah was content with what God gave him. He drank nothing but cold water.

Every day there was less and less water in the brook, for the sun dried it up, and there was no rain to fill it again. At last all the water was gone! What could Elijah do now? What use was food to eat, if he had nothing to drink? He would soon die of thirst. But his God remembered him, and told him to go to another place.

How much care God took of Elijah! At last He took him to heaven to live with Him. But you will be surprised to hear that Elijah never died. He was carried up to heaven by bright angels in a chariot of fire.

How wonderful! Why was God so very kind to Elijah? Why is God kind to anybody? We are all sinners, but God has given His only Son to die upon the cross that we may not be sent to hell. If you ask God to forgive you for Christ's sake He will do it, for He loves His Son Jesus Christ.

When a famine comes, those people whom God has forgiven need not be afraid. Here is a promise which God has made to them :—

'Behold, the eye of the Lord is upon them that fear Him, upon them that hope in His mercy; to deliver their souls from death, to keep them alive in famine.' (Ps. xxxiii, 18, 19.)

The history of Elijah and the ravens is written in 1 Kings xvii.

'From the glorious heaven,
　　Where the angels are,
God looks down on children,
　　Seeth them afar;
Heareth all they ask for,
　　All the night and day;
Watches, like a father,
　　All their work and play.

As a father giveth,
　　So He gives them bread;
Saves them out of danger,
　　Watches by their bed.
Tell all little children
　　Of their Father's care,
How He loves and pities
　　Children everywhere.'

Songs of Praise by Mrs. Bevan.

VII.

THE BURNING FIERY FURNACE.

THERE was a great **king** in Babylon, and this king had a great image made—a very tall image—as tall **as a** church-steeple, and **he** had made it of gold. Oh, what a rich king he must have been, and what a fine image! It was not set up in the town, but on a great plain, which was like a large field without hedges. There everybody could see the great image quite well.

The king desired all the lords, and **judges,** and captains in his kingdom to come to the plain.

When the rich lords were come together, **they** all stood round the image. There was a band of musicians there, with many kinds of instruments,—the harp with its sweet strings, the flute in which men breathe to make it sound, and many other instruments of which you have **never** heard. And the king was there, the proud king who did what he pleased.

A man cried out with a loud voice, 'As soon as the music begins to be played, then everybody is to bow down to the golden image that the king has set up; and if any one does not bow down, he shall be thrown immediately into a burning fiery furnace.'

Presently the music struck up, and the people fell down and worshipped the golden image.

Did I say that *all* the people bowed down to the golden image? *Almost* all — all but three.

Soon some of the king's servants came to him and said, 'O king, there are three men here who have not bowed down to the image. These men are not people of this land of Babylon — they are Jews.'

Then the king was in a great passion, for wicked people fall into passions just as little children do.

This king desired the three Jews to be brought to him.

When they came, he spoke very angrily to them, and said, 'Is it true you have not bowed down to the image? When you hear the music again will you fall down and worship the image? for if you will not, you shall be cast into a burning fiery furnace, and your God cannot deliver you out of it.'

But these three Jews were not frightened by the king's words. They said, 'We will not worship the image, and our God is able to deliver us from the burning fiery furnace, O king, and He will deliver us.'

Then the king was in a greater passion than before. To see his face it was terrible! for passion makes the face look very red and ugly.

But still the three Jews were not afraid.

The king desired that the furnace might be made seven times hotter than before.

Then he desired strong soldiers to cast the Jews into the flames.

These three good men had their legs and arms tied down, that they might not struggle when put in; and all their clothes were left on, their cloaks, and their turbans, and their stockings. Then the strong soldiers took hold of them and threw them into the fire, but the flames were so fierce that they caught hold of the soldiers and burnt them up.

What became of the poor Jews? They fell down in the midst of the furnace. Were they alive or dead?

The king came to look at the three Jews; but, oh, how much surprised he was to see them walking about in the fire, not only alive, but *loose!* for the fire had burned their bands, but not their clothes, nor their bodies. How wonderful!

But there was one thing which surprised the king still more. There were *four* men walking in the fire. The king called to his lords, and said, 'Did we not cast three men bound into the fire?' They said 'True, O king.' Then he said, 'I see *four* men loose, walking in the midst of the fire, and one of them is like the Son of God.'

Was He the Son of God? Oh, yes; for the Son of God loves us. God the Father had sent down His Son to save the three young Jews. How happy they were in the midst of the fire! They felt no pain.

Now the king saw that the God of the Jews could save them, and he came near to the door of the furnace (not so near as to be burned), and he called the three Jews by their names: 'Ye servants of the Most High God, come out, and come here.'

And they came out—yes, they walked out.

Then all the great lords came round them to see whether they were hurt; but there was not even the smell of fire on them; not one hair was singed, and their clothes were not even scorched.

Then the king began to praise their God, and to praise *them*, too, for not worshipping the image. And he sent round to all the towns in his kingdom, and desired that if anybody spoke against their God, he should be cut in pieces, and his house made into a heap of rubbish; for the king said, 'There 's no God who can deliver people like the God of these Jews.'

You will find the history of the three young Jews in Daniel iii.

'There is a happy land,
    Far far away,
Where saints in glory stand,
    Bright, bright as day.
Oh, how they sweetly sing,
" Worthy is our Saviour King:
Loud let His praises ring—
    Praise, praise for aye."

Come to this happy land,
    Come, come away ;
Why will ye doubting stand—
    Why still delay?
Oh, we shall happy be,
When from sin and sorrow free !
Lord, we shall live with thee—
    Blest, blest for aye.

Bright in that happy land
    Beams every eye—
Kept by a Father's hand,
    Love cannot die.
On, then, to glory run ;
Be a crown and kingdom won ;
And bright above the sun
    Reign, reign for aye.

A. YOUNG.
1838.

VIII.

THE DEN OF LIONS.

I AM going to tell you of a man who was shut up with a lion — not with one lion only, but with many lions — with hungry lions with open mouths, in the night, all alone, at the bottom of a deep den underground.

Why was he shut up there?

I will tell you why.

He had done nothing wicked. He was a very good man, who loved God, but there were some wicked men who hated him. There was a great king who was kind to the good man, and the wicked men did not like that. They wanted the king to be fond of *them*, but the king loved the good man best.

The good man's name was Daniel.

The wicked lords knew that Daniel prayed to the true God. As for them, they prayed to idols of wood and stone.

The wicked lords wanted to get good Daniel into disgrace with the king, so they made a very sly plan. They went to the king, and said, 'O king, do make a law that no one shall pray to any god, or to any body, for thirty days, except to you, O king; and do say that if anybody disobeys this law he shall be cast into the den of lions.' The king said he would make this law.

Daniel soon heard of this new law. Would he leave off praying to God for thirty days? Oh, no, not for one day. But perhaps he prayed when nobody saw him or heard him? No; he wished people to know that he prayed to God, that they might pray to Him too.

So he went into his room when the windows were open, and knelt down and prayed, morning, and noon, and evening. The wicked lords heard that Daniel went on praying, and they came to look at him, and when they had seen him on his knees speaking to God, then they went to the king.

They said to him, 'Did you not make a law that if anybody prayed to any god or any man for thirty days, he should be cast into the den of lions?'

'Yes,' said the king, 'I did; and I know I cannot change the law that I have made.' Then said the lords, 'That Daniel, though he has heard of this law, still goes on praying three times a-day.'

How sorry the king was when he heard this sad news! He loved Daniel, he could not bear to have him cast into the den. But what could he do?

It was not yet time to cast him in; the evening was the time; and till the evening came, and the sun had set, the king tried to think of some way of saving Daniel. But he could think of no way.

As soon as it was dark, the lords said, 'O king, you cannot change the law.' The king knew that, and he sent for Daniel and desired him to be cast into the den; but before he was put in, the king said to him, 'Your God will deliver you.' This was the only comfort the king had; he hoped that

the God of Daniel would save him from
the lions.

After Daniel had been thrown in, a great
stone was laid on the top of the den, and a
seal was put upon it, that nobody might
come in the night to take Daniel out, and
the king sealed the stone with his own seal.

What a miserable evening the king
passed! He could eat no supper. Usually
sweet music was played to him in the
evening, but he desired that the musicians
should not play; and when he went to bed
he could not sleep.

Very early in the morning he got up.
He went straight to the den, and he cried
out in a most sorrowful voice, 'O Daniel,
has your God whom you pray to been able
to deliver you from the lions?'

Oh, how the king did listen for the
answer! What if he should hear nothing
but the growls of the beasts!

But he heard a voice say, 'O king, live for
ever! My God has sent His angel, and has
shut the lions' mouths, and they have not
hurt me.'

On, how glad the king was!

Immediately he commanded the servants to take Daniel out of the den.

When Daniel came up, people looked to see whether the lions had bitten him, or scratched him, or bruised him. But no, there was not the least hurt found upon him. Most men would have been killed by the fright if they had been shut up with lions; but, no, Daniel had trusted in his God. He knew his God loved him and would save him.

What did the wicked lords say when they saw Daniel come up out of the den?

They had not much time to speak, for the king desired them to be cast into the den, and their wives and children with them. It was cruel to cast the poor wives in, and the little children, but as for these wicked men they well deserved to be eaten up.

Now it was seen how hungry the lions were, for before the men could get to the bottom of the den the lions sprang up and seized hold of them, and with their strong teeth smashed and crunched their bones to pieces. So, though the lions had gone without their supper, they had a good breakfast the next morning. God punishes wicked people when they have tried to hurt good people, and He often lets them fall into the very same trouble that they wanted to get the good people in. As it is written in the Bible, 'In the net which they hid is their own foot taken.' (Ps. ix, 15.)

The Bible tells us that Satan goes about like a roaring lion ready to devour us. But we must not be afraid, for God is much stronger than Satan, and He will keep us quite safe, as He kept Daniel, if we pray to Him as Daniel did.

This history is to be found in the Bible. See Daniel, vi.

'" Oh, mother!" cried a little chiid,
  " I cannot sleep to-night;
Hark! how the storm grows fierce and wild .
  It fills me with affright:
I hear the wind roar through the trees,
  And howl above my bed;
I tremble when it comes so near,
  And cover up my head."

" And why?" the mother **gently said,**
  " Why need you fear to sleep?
Why hide that little timid head?
  God will my darling keep.
What though the wind blows fierce and loud
  It can do us no ill;
We're in our Father's hand, and He
  Can bid the storm stand still.

Trust Him, **my child,** and peaceful rest.
  Safe in His tender care:
But think of others more distressed
  And breathe for them a prayer.
Think of the little sailor-boy,
  Tossing upon the deep;
Think **of** the wandering, homeless poor,
  Oh, pray for *them* — then SLEEP."'

                              M. S.

IX.

THE HEAVENLY BABE AND
ITS MOTHER.

DID you ever see an angel? I know you never did; neither did your father ever see an angel, nor your mother, nor your grandfather,—none of these ever saw an angel.

But some people have seen angels.

Angels are very bright creatures; they live in heaven with God, and they shine like the light. They know about us; they know that there is a world full of men, and women, and children. They pity us. Why? Because we are sinners. We do wrong things; we sin against God. Angels are not sinners. Though they have lived so many, many years with God, they have never done one wrong thing, and they never will.

Angels will always be happy. But shall we? We shall die one day. Shall we be happy after we are dead? Will God let

sinners live with Him? My dear child, did you ever think to yourself, 'Shall I go to heaven when I die?' There is a dreadful place called hell, and there are many sinners there, burning in the flames. You would not like to go there. I hope you will not.

I will now tell you what God has done for us miserable sinners.

A long while ago He told one of His bright angels to go on a message. He sent him from heaven to a poor woman named Mary. The angel's name was Gabriel.

What had Gabriel to say to Mary?

When the angel came into the place where Mary was, he told her the Lord was pleased with her, and was going to do her a great favour.

Was Mary delighted to hear this? No, she was frightened; she could not think what the angel meant.

Then the angel said, 'Fear not, Mary, for thou hast found favour with God.' Then the angel told her that she should soon have a little baby; and that He should be the Son

of God; and that His name should be
'Jesus.'

This was a very wonderful message. Why
was the Son of God to be a baby? God His
Father sent Him to be a baby, that He might
grow up to be a man, and then be punished
instead of us sinners. How good it was of
God to send His only Son to save us from
going to hell!

Mary believed what Gabriel told her.
Soon the angel went away.

At last the baby was born. Where do you
think it was born? You will be surprised
to hear—it was born in a stable.

Mary had taken a long journey with her
husband, Joseph; and when it was night
she went to the inn, but there was no room
for her there. There were so many travellers at the inn, that Mary and Joseph were
obliged to go into the stable. Among the
oxen and the asses the baby was born.

Mary wrapped Him in long clothes, and
laid Him in the manger. What a place for
the Son of God!

The children of kings lie in beautiful

cradles hung with muslin, and silk, and satin. But this baby was the Son of the King of kings, and He lay in a manger.

The people in the inn did not know that the Son of God was in the stable, but Mary knew who her babe was. She called Him her God and her Saviour; she knew He had come down from heaven to save her and many people.

You will like to see Mary in heaven Blessed was she among women. Of all the women who ever lived, she was the most blessed or happy. Jesus loved His mother very much, but He will love you as much if you wish to please God. He knows who wishes to please Him. He has said, ' Whosoever shall do the will of My Father which is in heaven, the same is My brother, and sister, and mother.'

Jesus has only one Father—God; but He has many brothers, and sisters, and mothers. There are a great many wicked people in this world who swear, and steal, and tell lies; but there are some who love God, and pray to Him, and believe in Him,

and try to please Him. Jesus counts them
His brothers, and sisters, and mothers.
Would you like to be the little brother
of the Lord Jesus? Would you like to be
His little sister? Luke, i, 26–35 ; ii. 1–7.

'Little children, God above,
In His tenderness and love,
  Has become a child like you.
See Him in the manger sleeping,
Weeping in this world of weeping
  For the evil that you do.

He hath left the world of light,
He hath left the angels bright :
  Seeking you—a child—He came,
Seek Him, children ; He is near:
Be His little angels here,
  Singing praises to His name.

Sweet Child Jesus, take my will,
Make it holy, pure, and still,
  Loving, meek, and undefiled.
From this evil world I flee,
Child of heaven, I seek but Thee;
  Thou dost love a little child.'

Songs of Eternal Life by Mrs. Bevan

X.

THE HAPPY NIGHT.

NEARLY two thousand years ago some good shepherds were in a field taking care of their flocks. It was night, and they were watching to prevent the wolves, and bears, and lions, coming to devour their pretty lambs and harmless sheep.

A very wonderful thing happened that night;— an angel came! What a glorious creature an angel is! Angels are bright like the sun, and their clothes are white like snow.

Yet when the shepherds saw this angel they were very much frightened. But the angel told them not to be afraid. 'Fear not,' he said; 'I bring you very joyful news. A baby is born this day, who is the Lord, and He is wrapped in long clothes: and He is lying in a manger.'

This was good news, indeed.

A long while before, God had promised

to send His own Son down from heaven to be a babe. And why? That He might die instead of us wicked creatures, and save us from going to hell. These shepherds had often heard of God's kind promise, and now the angel told them this babe was really born.

When the angel had done speaking, the most beautiful sight was seen. A number of angels suddenly appeared! How bright they must have shone in that dark night!

These angels began to sing. How sweet the sound must have been!

I can tell you the very words these angels sang. This was their song, 'Glory to God in the highest, and on earth peace, good-will towards men.'

It was because the Son of God was born that they sang this song—Jesus, the Son of God—He came to bring glory, and peace, and goodwill, and all happiness into this wicked world.

The angels did not stay very long.

See the good shepherds in the field alone with their sheep! What did they talk of now? Of that sweet babe who was lying in a manger. They knew He was in the next town, a very little way off, and they said one to another, 'Let us go and see Him.' So they left their sheep very quickly indeed.

There were other babies in Bethlehem, but most babies lie in soft cradles, or on their mothers' pillows; but there was no cradle and no pillow for this baby, only a manger full of straw or hay.

The shepherds found out in which stable the baby was, and they went in. And what did they see? There, in the midst of the oxen, and the cows, and the asses, they saw a babe, and near Him was His mother, a poor woman, named Mary. His father was in heaven, for God was His father; but there was a good man in the stable named Joseph, and he was the husband of Mary.

All kind people like to look on a little helpless infant. Do not you like to look at a baby, and to take it in your arms? But there never was such a baby as this. Though He was so weak and small, He was

the Son of God, and had made the world, and
the moon, and the stars.

How did the shepherds feel as they looked
at Him? They knew that baby loved them,
and had come down from heaven to save
them. Oh, how they loved that baby!

Did they take Him in their arms? Did
they kiss His sweet forehead? I cannot
tell you, for it is not written in the Bible.
The shepherds did not know all the pain
that tender babe would have to bear when
He was grown to be a man. Those little
hands with fingers folded up, afterwards
had nails thrust through them; and those
tender feet, which had never touched the
ground, were afterwards fastened to the
cross of wood. Oh, to have looked upon
that babe, and to have thought of all it
would suffer, might have made the hardest
heart feel sorry! But that babe is happy
now—oh, very happy! After dying upon
the cross He was made alive again, and He
went up into heaven, and there He is now,
and the shepherds with Him, singing the
angels' song. One day He will come to

this world again, shining brighter than angels do; and the shepherds will come with Him, and all people who have ever loved Him.

Those shepherds often talked about Jesus, they told everybody about the babe in the manger, and about the angels in the sky, and they praised God with all their hearts for having let them see and hear such wonderful things.

You have *heard* about the babe in the manger, though you have not seen Him. There are many children who have never heard about Him. God has been very kind to you in letting *you hear* about Him. I hope you love Jesus. Some children do. If they were to die, the angels would come and fetch their souls to be with Jesus in heaven.

This history is written in Luke, ii, 8-20.

F

' Once in Royal David's city
  Stood a lowly cattle-shed,
Where a mother laid her baby,
  In a manger for His bed.
Mary was that mother mild:
Jesus Christ her little child.

He came down to earth from heaven,
  Who is God and Lord of all,
And His shelter was a stable,
  And His stable was a stall.
With the poor, and mean, and lowly,
Lived on earth our Saviour holy.

And through all His wondrous childhood
  He would honour and obey,
Love and watch the lowly mother,
  In whose gentle arms He lay.
Christian children all should be
Mild, obedient, good as He.'

            MRS. C. F. ALEXANDER.

XI.

THE OLD MAN AND THE BABY.

MOST children love little babies. A babe of six weeks old is very little indeed ; it cannot sit up ; it lies down in its mother's arms, and its head rests upon her hand ; it can open its eyes and look about, and it is pleased with the light of the candle ; but it does not know its mother from a stranger, and it will go to anybody without being frightened ; it smiles, but it never laughs, though it often cries.

I am now going to tell you about the sweetest baby of six weeks old that was ever seen in this world. Who was this baby ? Was He a prince, the son of a king, or of a queen ? He was not called a prince, yet He was greater than any prince in this world.

Who was this baby ? He was the Son of God. He came down from heaven to be a baby. And why ?—that He might grow

to be a man, and then die upon the cross of
wood for our sins! Oh, how kind to come
down to die for *us* that we might not be
punished! But I am not going to tell you
now about His dying, but about His being a
little baby.

The name of His mother was Mary,—she
was a good woman; the name of His Father
was God. Mary had a husband called
Joseph, and He was very kind to this sweet
baby.

The baby was born in a stable, but when
He was nearly six weeks old His mother took
Him a little journey; she went to a town
eight miles off, called Jerusalem.

She went in the beautiful place there
called the Temple, where people often
prayed to God, as they do in church. She
took her little baby in her arms when she
went to the Temple. Joseph was with
her.

Why did Mary take her baby to the
Temple? To give Him to God, because
He was her first child. And she brought
with her two young pigeons, to give them

to God. They were to be killed and burnt, but the baby was not to be killed.

When Mary was in the Temple, an old man came in. Who was this old man? He was a very good man, and his name was Simeon. When men are old their hair turns white like silver, and their backs are bent, and their knees are weak, and they cannot walk fast; but good old men are very happy. They know that they shall soon die, and they are not afraid, for they wish to be with God. Simeon knew he should soon die, but God had promised him that before he died he should see the Son of God.

When Mary brought her baby into the Temple, God told Simeon to go in and look at His Son. How glad Simeon was to go!

As soon as he saw Mary he knew who she was, and who her baby was. He took Him up in his arms, and began to pray to God.

Would you not have liked to see that good old man praying to God, and holding that lovely infant in his arms? He told God that he was now ready to die, because he had seen the Saviour of all people in the world. He said, 'Lord, now lettest Thou Thy servant depart and in peace; for mine eyes have seen Thy SALVATION' (that is, the *Saviour*).

Mary and Joseph, who were standing by, were much surprised to hear what the old man said.

Simeon then began to talk to Mary, and told her a great deal more about her child.

While he was speaking an old woman came in. I believe she was more than a hundred years old, and she had been a widow for a very long while indeed. She lived close to the Temple, and was very fond of being there, and of praying to God. Her name was Anna.

When she saw the baby, she began to praise God for having sent His Son from heaven to save people from going to hell.

There were other people in the Temple who heard what Anna said, and who were glad to think that the Saviour was come.

Would you like to see that baby? You

can never see the BABY, but you may see the SON OF GOD. He is in heaven now with His Father, and He will come one day into the world, and THEN you will see Him.

You may read the history of Simeon in Luke, ii, 22–38.

> ' Little child, do you love Jesus?
>> Oh, how He loves!
> Do you wish to go to heaven?
>> Oh, how He loves!
> First of all ask His forgiveness,
> With your heart, although quite helpless;
> Jesus little children blesses:
>> Oh, how He loves!
>
> He will listen to your prayer:
>> Oh, how He loves!
> Feed you by His tender care:
>> Oh, how He loves!
> He became a child just like you;
> Here He suffered to redeem you,
> And at last He died to save you:
>> Oh, how He loves!
>
>> *Writer unknown.*

XII.

THE KING OF THE JEWS.

THERE was once a wicked man who was King of the Jews, his name was Herod: he lived at Jerusalem.

One day some men came to his city and said, 'Where is He that is born King of the Jews? For we have seen His star in the east, and are come to worship Him.'

But was not Herod king of the Jews? Yes, he was; but a little baby had been born whom God sent to be King of the Jews. This baby was the Son of God. Very few people knew anything about Him. But God had made a star shine in the sky to show these men where His Son was born.

These men were wise men; they had learned a great deal. They were good men also, for they loved the Son of God, and wanted to see Him. They had come a great way on purpose to find Him. They

knew He was somewhere near Jerusalem, but they did not know exactly where; so they asked everybody, 'Where is the King of the Jews?'

King Herod heard that some wise men had come from a long way off, and were asking for the King of the Jews. Herod was very sorry to hear this; he did not like hearing of another king. He did not know where the King of the Jews was, but he asked some of his friends to look in the Bible to see where God had said He should be born. They looked, and they found that God had written in His book that the King of the Jews should be born in a place called Bethlehem.

Herod was glad to find out where this king was born, and hecalled the wise men, and he told them that this little king was born at Bethlehem. He said to them, 'Go, and look for the young child, and when you nave found Him come and tell me, that I may come and worship Him.' But did Herod wish to worship this little king? Oh, no, he wanted to kill Him! but he pretended to love Him, that he might find out which child He was.

The wise men believed what Herod said, and they meant to come back and tell him.

They went to Bethlehem; they had only seven miles to go. But how could they find out the little king? God made the star to shine again in the sky; the star moved along, and showed the wise men the way, and at last it stopped just over a house in Bethlehem. Oh, how very glad the wise men were to see the star again! They went into the house, and they found there a young child about a year old. He was the King of the Jews; He was the Son of God, and had come down from God His Father, in heaven, to be a baby. And why? That when He was a man He might die upon the cross to save us from going to hell. Oh, how kind He was!

The baby's mother was with Him in the house.

Joseph, Mary's husband, was with the babe. He took care of Mary, and helped her to bring up the glorious little King Jesus.

The first thing the wise men did was to worship Him, because they knew He was the Son of God.

These wise men were rich : they had brought beautiful things with them from their own land ; they made presents to the king ; they opened their boxes, or bags, or baskets, and they took out the most precious thing in the world — gold ; they also took out sweet-smelling gums, which flow from trees ; these are called frankincense and myrrh. Mary was very poor, but God had sent her some gold.

The wise men remembered what Herod had said. They meant to go back and tell him they had found the child. But they had a dream, and in the dream God told them not to go back to Herod ; so they went back to their own country, and they did not go back to Jerusalem.

Happy wise men ! they saw the Lord of glory ! Could they ever forget that sweet, that lovely baby ? But He is more lovely now. He is in heaven, on the throne with God, and He will come down here some day shining brighter than the sun.

But what did wicked Herod do when he found the wise men did not come back?

He was very angry. He was a very passionate man, and when he was angry everybody might well be frightened. Herod said, 'I will kill all the babies in Bethlehem, then I shall be sure to kill this young king amongst the rest.' What a cruel man this Herod was!

He sent his soldiers to Bethlehem to kill all the little children of one year old. It was of no use for mothers to hide their babies, the soldiers would find them out. It was of no use for mothers to hold their babies fast, the soldiers would pull them away. Oh, what screams, what bitter sobs, must have been heard that day! Do you not pity the poor mothers of Bethlehem?

And did Mary lose her baby, and was the Son of God killed? Oh, no. Before Herod sent his men, God had sent an angel to Bethlehem. He came one night to Joseph, and said to him, 'Take the young child and His mother, and go into Egypt, and stay there till I tell you to come back, for Herod will try to kill the young child.' So Joseph got up that night, and told Mary to get up, and to bring the baby with her; and they all set out that night upon their long journey.

Herod did not know that the little king was gone away, and that it was no use to kill all the babies in Bethlehem.

God knows what wicked men will do.

No one could kill the Son of God till He chose to die.

He is the King of the Jews, and He is the King of all people.

You may read this history in Matthew, ii. 1-16.

'Around the throne of God in heaven
　　Thousands of children stand,—
Children whose sins are all forgiven,
　　A holy, happy band,
　　　　Singing, Glory, glory, glory.

In flowing robes of spotless white
　　See every one arrayed,
Dwelling in everlasting light,
　　And joys that never fade,
　　　　Singing, Glory, glory.

Once they were little things like you,
　　And lived on earth below,
And could not praise, as now they do,
　　The Lord who loved them so,
　　　　Singing, Glory, glory.

What brought them to that world above
　　That heaven so bright and fair,
Where all is peace, and joy, and love?
　　How came those children there,
　　　　Singing, Glory, glory?

Because the Saviour shed His blood
　　To wash away their sin:
Bathed in that pure and precious flood
　　Behold them white and clean,
　　　　Singing, Glory, glory.'

XIII.

THE HEAVENLY BOY.

ONCE there was a boy who came down from heaven; He was the Son of God, and He is called the Lord Jesus Christ. The people in the town where He lived did not know that He was the Lord. They knew His name was Jesus, but they did not call Him the Lord Jesus, but only Jesus.

He was a poor boy, and lived with a man called Joseph, who was a carpenter. Joseph was not His father. God was His Father.

He had a mother named Mary; she was a very good woman; she knew her little son came down from heaven. No mother ever had such a son as the Lord Jesus. He always minded what she said; He always behaved well to her, and treated her kindly.

In the spring, all the men in the land went up to Jerusalem. When they got there they used to meet together in a room, and eat a roasted lamb, and sing hymns, and pray to God. It was very pleasant to go to this feast. Very often the fathers took their children with them, and sometimes the mothers went too.

When Jesus was twelve years old, He went up to Jerusalem with Joseph and Mary, and with their neighbours who lived in their town. He stayed there about a week.

At the end of that time Joseph and Mary set out with their neighbours to return home to their own town. Did Jesus go home with them? No, He did not: but Joseph and Mary did not miss Him at first: they thought He was with some neighbours, walking on a little before, or coming after them. But when the evening came they did not see Him, and they began to be frightened. They asked all their neighbours where He was, but nobody knew. What could they do? They said they would turn back and look for Him at Jerusalem. They did not find Him on the road.

At last they came to Jerusalem; they

looked everywhere for Jesus. At last they found Him. Where was He? In the Temple. What was He doing there? He was among the children who were being taught.

There were some wise men in Jerusalem who used to teach the boys about God and about the Bible. Jesus was at the Temple hearing these wise men teach. When they asked Him questions, He gave very good answers. Then He asked them questions. Teachers like to hear children ask questions · it shows that they wish to understand and to grow wise.

Should you not like to know what questions Jesus asked? I should; but I do not know. But this I do know, that both His questions and His answers were so wise, that His teachers were quite surprised. They had never taught such a child. There never was such a child before, for this was the only child who was the Son of God.

Joseph and Mary were very much surprised to find Jesus in the Temple. His mother said to Him, 'Son, why have you done so? Your father and I have been looking for you, and we have been very unhappy about you.' Then Jesus answered, 'Why did you look for Me? Do you not know that I must do My Father's business?'

Whom did He call His Father? Not Joseph, but God in heaven—He was His Father. Jesus came down from heaven to please His Father.

When He was a little boy He knew that one day He should be nailed to a cross. Other boys do not know what will happen to them when they grow up, but Jesus knew everything. Many boys think that they shall be very happy as soon as they are men, that they shall do what they like, and not mind anybody. But Jesus thought only about minding His heavenly Father

Oh, how much I wish you would try to be like Him! Jesus would be pleased if He saw you wishing to be such a child as He was. When you are going to do what is wrong, ask yourself this question: 'Did Jesus behave in this way when He was a

boy?' Then ask **God to make you** like
Jesus. Luke, ii. 41–50.

'Jesus, who reigns above the **sky,**
And keeps the world in awe,
Was once a child as young as **I,**
And kept **His Father's** law.

At twelve years old He talked with men
(The Jews all wondering stand);
Yet He obeyed His mother then,
And came at her command.'

WATTS

HAPPY CHILDREN.

'As we play at evening
Round our fathers' knees,
Birds are not so merry,
Singing in the trees.

Lambs are not so happy,
'Mid the meadow flowers;
They have play and pleasure.
But not love like ours.

For the heart that's loving,
Works of love will do;
Those we dearly **cherish**
We must honour too.

To our fathers' teaching
Listen day **by** day,
And our mothers' bidding
Cheerfully obey.'

MRS. C. F. ALEXANDER.

XIV.

THE HEAVENLY DOVE

Do you remember the first time you went to church or chapel? You saw a man standing in a pulpit in the midst of the church; you heard him speak loud, so that everybody could hear him. That man was the preacher.

I am now going to tell you of a preacher who did not stand in a pulpit; he did not preach in a church or a chapel, but out of doors; he did not preach in the streets, but in the country far away among the green hills. His name was John. He wore very coarse clothes, and he had a leather band round his waist. He lived in a place called a desert, where there were no houses, and he ate the honey that he found in the holes of the rocks.

A great many people came to hear John. What did John say to them? He said, 'Repent.' What does that mean? It means, 'Turn from your wicked ways.' John told the people that God hated sin — all kinds of sin, stealing, lying, swearing, and fighting.

Some of the people wished to turn from their sins and to please God. Then John took them to the edge of the water, and told them to go in. Why did he tell them to go in? Not to make their bodies clean, but to show them how God would make their hearts clean from sin. This was called 'baptizing,' John baptized everybody who was sorry for their sins.

Among the people who came to be baptized, at last there came one who had never done anything wrong. Who could that be? All men have done wrong many times, but this man was the Son of God; He had come down from heaven that He might save us from going to hell. His name was Jesus.

After Jesus had been baptized in the water, just as He was coming out of it, and as He was praying to His Father, a very wonderful thing happened,— the heavens were opened. How bright it would be if we could see the place where God the Father lives beyond the sky! This is what John saw. Out of the heavens there came the Holy Spirit of God. He came down like a dove, and rested upon Jesus. Oh, what a lovely sight! Then a voice was heard,—it was the voice of God the Father in heaven; He said, 'This is My dear Son; I am pleased with Him.'

Would you not have liked to be there to see the Son of God, and the Spirit of God, and to hear the voice of God the Father.

I hope you will one day see that glorious sight and hear that heavenly voice.

Perhaps you feel, 'I am a wicked child; I am not fit to live with God.'

Well, I am glad if you feel you are a sinner. But do not be afraid; Jesus can wash away all your sins and make your heart clean.

I know you wish to be happy: you may be happy.

There are fierce beasts called lions, tigers, wolves, and bears. Perhaps you have seen them shut up in cages. Wicked people are like wild beasts.

There is a gentle bird called a dove. It is a sweet, harmless creature. The Holy Spirit of God is like this dove. If this Holy Spirit were to come into your heart, you would grow gentle, like a dove.

But will the Holy Spirit come? Yes, Jesus has promised to send Him into the hearts of all people who ask Him. What a happy child you might be if your sins were forgiven, if your heart was made clean, and if the heavenly dove was with you!— Should you not be happy? Oh, yes; even *now* you would be happy. But you would be happier still one day, for one day you would live with God.

Read this history in Matt. iii, 13-17; Mark, i, 9-11; Luke, iii, 21, 22.

A CHILD'S PRAYER.

' Lord. teach a little child to pray,
Thy grace betimes impart,
And grant Thy Holy Spirit may
Renew my infant heart.'

JANE TAYLOR

XV.

CHRIST IN THE WILDERNESS.

THERE is one who goes about teaching men to be wicked.

Who is that? It is not a person you can see. No, he has not a body like yours; but he has a mind, and a wicked mind. His name is Satan, and he is often called the devil. He is very miserable, and he tries to make everybody miserable. He often puts it into the mind of a boy to wish to steal. When a boy sees nice rosy apples hanging on a tree, the devil says, 'Take them, they are so nice; nobody will see you.'

But we ought not to please the devil, but to please God. It is God who made us, and we ought to obey Him. When the devil wants you to be naughty, then say to God, Oh, keep me from sin.'

Is there anybody who has never done what Satan wished? No; everybody has done many wrong things. Have not you? have you never been disobedient? O yes— you have been naughty very often. And why? Is it because Satan tempts you? That is *one* reason. But there is another; you have a naughty heart. There once was a man in this world who had *not* a naughty heart, and He never did one wrong thing. This man was the Son of God. He came down to live here for a little while, and then to die; His name was Jesus. He knew we were wicked, and must be punished, so He said He would be punished instead of us. But He was not wicked like us. Satan wanted to make Him wicked, but He never could.

Once Jesus went into a place quite alone; it was called a wilderness. Nobody lived there; there were no corn-fields nor fruit-trees, nor sheep nor cows—only lions and bears, who howled and roared; and there were stones upon the ground, not flowers— and there were deep pits, but no rivers, nor running brooks—and there were stinging scorpions and biting serpents. Jesus was a long while in this horrible place quite alone, and all the time He ate no bread and drank no water. He was there forty days without eating or drinking anything. You would die very soon if you had nothing to eat; you would not live for four days, perhaps—you would *certainly* die in seven days. But Jesus lived forty days without food. It was God His Father who kept Him alive.

At last Jesus was very hungry, and then the devil came to Him. And did he dare to speak to the Son of God? Oh, yes. I told you he was very bold. He said, 'Why do you not make these stones into bread?' Jesus *could* make stones into bread, but He *would* not, because His Father had not told Him. So, though He was very hungry, He would not make the stones into bread.

The devil then tried another plan. He took Jesus to the top of a very high place. Have you ever been to the top of a church? It was to such a high place that Satan took Jesus; it was the top of the Temple, when he asked Jesus to throw Himself down from the top. Satan said, 'God will tell His angels to keep you from being hurt.'

But it is very wicked to throw ourselves down from high places, and Jesus would not do it.

Then the devil took Him to the top of a very high mountain.

Were you ever at the top of a high mountain? There are some mountains five miles high, and it would take you two days to climb up to the top; but I do not think a child like you could get up at all.

Jesus did not climb up this mountain. Satan took Him there all at once. Jesus let Satan take Him there.

No one ever saw so many beautiful sights as Jesus saw from the top of this mountain. He saw all the most beautiful things in the world, such as grand houses, and sweet gardens, and armies of soldiers, and ships with flags, and carriages with horses, and tables covered with gold and silver cups, and thrones of ivory where kings sit, and crowns of jewels which kings wear.

H

Then the devil said to Jesus, 'I will give you all these things, for they are all mine, and I give them to whom I will.'

Was that true?

Oh, no! the devil knew it was not true,—everything belongs to God, for everything was made by Him.

Then Satan promised Jesus to give Him all these grand things if He would kneel down and worship him like God.

Would Jesus do that?

No, He would worship no one but God His Father.

When the devil found he could not make Jesus do one wicked thing he went away.

But Jesus was very hungry—God His Father knew that, and He sent His angels to feed Him.

How glad I am that Jesus did not do what Satan asked! If Jesus had been wicked like us, He could not have saved us from going to hell to be with the devil, but now He can.

Believe in Him and you shall be saved.

God wishes to save you, Jesus wishes to

save you, but the devil wishes to torment
you.   Matt. iv. 1–11.

Happy the children who are gone
  To live with Jesus Christ in peace,
Who stand around His glorious throne,
  Redeemed by blood, and saved by grace.

The Saviour, whom they loved below,
  Hath kindly wiped their tears away;
No sin, no sorrow, there they know,
  But dwell in one eternal day.

There to their golden harps they sing,
  While tens of thousands join their songs,
Hosannas to the immortal King,
  To whom immortal praise belongs.

O glorious Lord, and when shall we
  Be brought with them in bliss to join,
Thy lovely countenance to see,
  And sing Thy mercies all divine?'
                              Writer unknown.

XVI.

THE HEAVENLY LAMB.

Did you ever spend a happy day? Perhaps you will answer, 'I have spent a great many happy days.' What made those days so happy? Was it that you went a journey into the country? or that you went to a feast under the trees? or that you went to see your little cousins? I do not know what made you happy on your happy days, but I will tell you of a happier day than any you have spent.

Once there was a good man who preached to a great many people.

His name was John; there were some men who liked to be with him, and these men were called his disciples.

One day he was standing in the country with two of his disciples, when he saw a man walking along a little way off.

When John saw this man he looked at Him, and then said to his disciples, 'See the Lamb of God.'

What did John mean? Was it a lamb he saw? No, it was a man.

Why did he call Him a lamb? I will tell you why.

That man was God as well as man; He was the Son of God.

The Son of God was like a sweet and gentle lamb, and was willing to die for us, though He had done no sin. How much pleased John was to see Him? John loved Him, and He wished his disciples to love Him too.

One of those two disciples was called Andrew. I do not know the name of the other.

If you had been Andrew, what would you have done when you heard John say, 'Behold the Lamb of God?'

I think I hear you answer, 'I would have gone after that gentle Lamb.'

That is what Andrew did, and the other disciple too. The two disciples went after the Son of God.

While they were walking behind Him,

Jesus turned and said to them, 'What is it you want?'

How kind it was of the Son of God to speak to these poor men!

They answered, 'Master, where do you live?'

Jesus said, 'Come and see.'

Was not this kind?

The two men went to the house where Jesus lived. Did He ask them to come in? Yes, He did, and He let them stay with Him all the rest of the day.

Must not *that* have been a happy day? It was a day spent with the Son of God.

I have a little more to tell you about Andrew. He loved Jesus so much, that he wanted his brother to know him too. He had a brother called Simon, and he said to him, 'We have found the Christ.' It was Jesus that he meant; he called Him the Christ.

Simon did not know where Jesus lived, but Andrew did. and he showed his brother the way. How pleasant it is when brothers are kind to each other!

As soon as Jesus saw Simon, He knew who he was without being told, and He knew the name of his father, too, and He said, 'Thou art Simon, the son of Jonas.'

Jesus knows the name of every one. He knows your name, and your father's name, and your mother's name.

Jesus gave Simon a new name; He called him Peter. Why? There is a meaning in the word Peter; it means, 'Stone.' Christ knew that Simon would be like a stone. Is it good to be like a stone? Yes, it is good to be *firm* like a stone. Jesus knew that Peter would stand *firm* one day when wicked people would try to turn him away from God.

We ought all to be like stones in standing firm, for it is a dreadful thing to turn away from Jesus.

Wicked boys may laugh at you, and try to persuade you not to mind Jesus. But ask God to give you His Spirit, to keep you *firm* and faithful unto death. John, i. 29–42.

THE HEAVENLY LAMB.

‘ I love the Lamb who died for me
I love His little lamb to be ;
I love the Bible, where I find
How good my Saviour was, and kind ;
I love beside His cross to stay,
I love the grave where Jesus lay :
I love His people and their ways,
I love with them to pray and praise ;
I love the Father and the Son,
I love the Spirit He sent down :
I love to think the time will come,
When I shall be with Him at home.’

XVII.

THE MAN UNDER THE TREE:
OR, NATHANAEL.

NATHANAEL was a good man. He lived in those days when the Lord Jesus was walking about this world. Did Nathanael see Him? Yes, he did.

Nathanael had a friend named Philip. These two friends, Nathanael and Philip, had often heard the Bible read out aloud. There was one promise in the Bible which they had taken much notice of,—it was this, that God would one day send His Son into the world. Nathanael and Philip thought this a great promise, and they wished to know the Son of God.

One day Philip came to Nathanael and said, 'We have found Him; it is Jesus of Nazareth.'

Was this true? Oh, yes; Jesus of Nazareth was the Son of God. At first Nathanael thought that Philip had made a mistake, and that he had not really found the Son of God. Nathanael had heard that a great many wicked people lived in Nazareth, and he thought that the Son of God could not come from such a wicked city; so he replied, 'Can any good thing come out of Nazareth?'

Philip gave a very short answer,— it was this, 'Come and see.'

Philip knew where to find Jesus, and he took Nathanael with him.

At last the two friends came within sight of Jesus.

Did the Lord know who that man was walking with Philip?

Oh, yes, He knew who he was; He had made him; He knew all about him.

As soon as He saw him coming near, he said, 'Behold an Israelite indeed, in whom there is no guile, or deceit.'

What did He mean by an Israelite?

There was once a good man called Israel who prayed very earnestly. Nathanael was

like that Israel, for he had prayed earnestly, and so he was an Israelite indeed.

But he was quite surprised to hear Jesus speak of him as if He knew him, and he cried out, 'How do you know me?'

Then Jesus answered, 'Before Philip called thee, when thou wast under the fig-tree I saw thee.'

Had Nathanael been alone under a fig-tree? Yes.

Jesus had seen Nathanael hid under the thick branches of a shady fig-tree, when no one else saw him, and we may be quite sure that He saw him praying and asking God to forgive his sins.

Nathanael knew that no one but God had seen him under the fig-tree; so, when he heard what Jesus said, he knew that He was God; and he cried out, 'Master, Thou art the Son of God, Thou art the King of Israel.' How happy Nathanael was to find the Saviour!

Jesus soon made him such a sweet promise! He said, 'One day thou shalt see the angels of God going up and coming down upon the Son of man.' What did this mean? That Nathanael should one day see Jesus go up to heaven with angels.

Yes, and he did see that. But it means also that Nathanael shall see Jesus coming again with angels. And he shall see *that;* for Nathanael will come with Him.

And would you, dear child, like to come with Jesus and the angels, and be an angel too?

If you would, then go like Nathanael and pray all alone by yourself.

Look for Nathanael's history in John, i. 43–51.

> ' We're travelling home to heaven above;
> > Will you go?
> To sing the Saviour's dying love;
> > Will you go?
> Millions have reached that blessed shore,
> Their trials and labours all are o'er,
> But still there's room for millions more;
> > Will you go?
>
> We're going to walk the plains of light;
> > Will you go?
> Far, far from death, and curse, and night;
> > Will you go?

The crown of life we then shall wear,
The conqueror's palm we then shall bear,
And all the joys of heaven share:

Will you go?

We're going to see the bleeding Lamb;
Will you go?
With joyful songs to praise His name;
Will you go?
Our sun will then no more go down,
Our moon no more will be withdrawn,
Our days of mourning past and gone;
Will you go?

The way to heaven is straight and plain!
Will you go?
Repent, believe, be born again;
Will you go?
The Saviour cries aloud to thee,
" Take up thy cross and follow Me,"
And thou shalt My salvation see;
Will you go?

Oh, could I hear some sinner say,
" I will go."
Oh, could I hear him humbly pray,
" Make me go."
And all his old companions tell,
" I will not go with you to hell,
I long with Jesus Christ to dwell:
Let me go."

I

'I have a Father in the promised land,
I have a Father in the promised land,
My Father calls me; I must go,
To meet Him in the promised land;
I'll away, I'll away to the promised land;
My Father calls me; I must go,
To meet Him in the promised land.

I have a Saviour in the promised land,
I have a Saviour in the promised land,
My Saviour calls me; I must go,
To meet Him in the promised land,
I'll away, I'll away to the promised land;
My Saviour calls me; I must go,
To meet Him in the promised land.'

XVIII.

THE WOMAN AT THE WELL.

I AM now going to tell you of a poor man who travelled on foot. Where was He going? Was it to His home? He had none. He was always going from place to place to teach people about God.

The poor man did not travel alone: there were twelve other poor men who went with Him; they were His friends; they liked to be with Him, and to hear what He said about God and heaven.

One day this poor man was making a journey with His friends. It was very hot, and about the middle of the day: He was tired, and hungry, and thirsty; He saw a well of water just under a hill, and He sat down by it to rest Himself. There was a town a little way off, and His friends went to the town to buy some food, so that the poor man was all alone by the side of the well; but though He was thirsty He could not drink, for the well was deep, and there was no bucket there.

Very soon a woman came to the well with a pail to fetch water; then the poor man said to her, 'Give Me to drink.'

She saw that this poor man was a Jew, and she did not like Jews. I hope *you* do, for God loves the poor Jews. The woman would not give the thirsty traveller any water because He was a Jew.

Was the poor man angry? Oh, no; He was a meek, gentle, and patient man; He only answered the woman, ' If you had asked *Me* for some water, I would have given you running spring water.'

The woman was surprised to hear this. 'How could you give me water,' she said, 'when you have no jug or bucket, and the well is deep?' Then she began to say what good water there was in the well, and that she was sure the poor man could not give her any better water.

But the poor man told her that He could give her better water than *that*: 'for,' said He, 'any one who drinks this water is

soon thirsty again, but if any one drink of the water I give, he is never thirsty any more.'

Then the woman thought she would like such water as that, for she could not bear the trouble of coming to the well every day to fill her pail; so she said, ' *Sir*, do give me some of this water, that I may never thirst or come here to fetch water.'

But instead of giving her any water, the poor man began to talk to her about her sins, for He knew she was a wicked woman, and had done many wrong things.

She was quite surprised to find that the stranger knew all about her. She exclaimed, ' I see you are a prophet.' But still she did not guess who He was.

At last He told her; and who do you think that poor man was? The Son of God! Oh, wonderful! The Son of the Great God —a poor man sitting by a well! It is wonderful, yet it is true.

When the woman knew that it was Jesus Christ who was talking to her, she left her pail and ran very quickly into the town.

What for ? To call the people to see the
Lord Jesus Christ. She said to them,
'Come and see a man who has told me
everything I have done.'

The people of the town went back with
the woman to the well.

The poor man was still sitting by the
well, and His twelve friends were with
Him. But He had not eaten any dinner
—He could not, for He was so glad about
this woman and about the people of the
town, for He was going to teach them,
and to save their souls. He liked saving souls. It was His delight. He had
come down from heaven on purpose to save
us.

The people from the town begged Him
not to go on His journey, but to stay with
them : so He went to the town and stayed
there two days. How much He talked to
the people while He was there ! He told
them about God His Father, and about sin,
and Satan, and how He was going to save
them by dying for them.

A great many of the people believed what

He said, and loved Him.   Some people had
not believed when the woman said, 'He
has told me all that ever I did.'   But they
did believe when they heard Him speak
themselves.   '*Now*,' they said, 'we do
believe that this is the Saviour of the
world.'

Did the poor man give water to the
people? Yes, He gave them water from
heaven.   What do I mean by 'water?'
The Holy Spirit of God.

When people have the Holy Spirit in their
hearts they are happy, for then they love
God.   People who do not love God are not
happy ; they are always trying to be happy,
but they *cannot* be happy.   Can money
make people happy? No.   Can cakes and
fruit? Can new coats and frocks? Can
picture-books? Can fine sights? None of
these things can make you happy *always*.
They please for a little while, but the pleasure is soon over.   But if you love God you
will always be happy — you will thirst no
more.

Should you like to be happy? I know

you would. Then go to Jesus. He is not sitting by a well now, yet you may find Him, though you cannot see Him. He is sitting on a throne in heaven. If you were to speak to Him He would hear you. Say to Him, 'O Lord Jesus, make me happy. Give me Thy Holy Spirit. I want to live with God, and not to go to hell.' John, iv. 5–42.

'Like mist on the mountain,
  Like ships on the sea,
So swiftly the years
  Of our pilgrimage flee.
In the grave of our fathers
  How soon shall we lie!
Dear children, to-day
  To a Saviour fly!

How sweet are the flowerets
  In April and May,!
But often the frost makes
  Them wither away.
Like flowers you may fade:
  Are you ready to die?
While 'yet there is room'
  To a Saviour fly.'

ROBERT M'CHEYNE.

XIX.

THE FOUR FISHERMEN.

THERE were once four fishermen, two of them were brothers, and the other two were brothers. Two brothers were called John and James, and two brothers were called Andrew and Simon Peter. These four fishermen were friends; they shared with each other all they caught, for they were partners in trade. They had two little ships; one ship belonged to John and James, and the other to Peter and Andrew.

The best time for fishing is in the night. These young men used to go fishing in the night. They went one night in their two little ships to catch fish, but they could not catch any at all. In the morning they left their ships and went on shore, where they began to wash their nets.

There came to the place where they were, a man whom they knew well and loved much. He was greater than any man upon earth, yet He was the friend of the fishermen. He looked like a poor man, yet He had made all things.

Who could this be?

It was Jesus Christ, the Son of God. He had come down from heaven to live in the world a little while. He preached very often to poor people. Now He was standing by the sea-side, and a great crowd of people were standing round Him.

Jesus wished to get out of the crowd, that He might preach to them more easily. He saw the two ships; He knew whose ships they were. He saw Simon Peter very near washing his net, and He said He would go into his ship, and He told Simon to push it a little way into the water.

When He was got into the ship, He sat down and preached to the people who were standing on the land. Now they could hear Him very well, and they could see Him better than before.

The two brothers, Simon and Andrew, were in the ship with Jesus. These poor men must have felt tired after the sleepless night they had passed. Jesus knew all their

troubles without their telling Him, for He knew all things, because He was God.

After He had done preaching He said to Simon, 'Make your ship go further into the water, and then let down your nets to catch fish.'

Simon said, 'We have been trying all night to catch fish and have not caught any, but we will do what you tell us to do.'

The Lord Jesus was pleased with Simon for doing what He told him.

Simon and Andrew let down their net, and then tried to pull it up again, but in trying to pull it up, the net broke.

What could they do now? All their fishes would soon get out of the net if they did not make haste.

They made a sign to John and James, who were in the other ship, to come and help them. Then all the four fishermen lifted up the net and took the fishes out of it; and there were so many that both the ships were filled, and were so heavy that they were beginning to sink.

Then it was that Simon Peter fell down

at the knees of Jesus, who was sitting in the ship, and said, 'Go away from me, for I am a sinful man.'

Why did he ask Jesus to go away from him? Did he not love Him? Had not Jesus been very kind to him in letting him catch all these fish? Yes, and that was the reason that Simon asked Him to go away, for he felt that he was not good enough to have such a friend.

Did Jesus go away from him? Oh, no; He knew that Peter loved Him. He said to him, 'Fear not; from this time thou shalt catch men.'

What did He mean by catching men? He meant that Peter would catch the *souls* of men. He meant that Peter would tell men that Jesus was come down from heaven to die for their sins upon the cross and save them from going to hell. Afterwards Peter was a preacher, and a great many men believed what he said, and turned to God, and were saved. So he did catch men, and so did Andrew, and John, and James: these four fishermen left off fishing and became preachers

When they had brought their two ships to land they left them, and went after Jesus. They followed Him from place to place, and listened to His kind voice and saw the wonders He did.

It is a happy thing to belong to Jesus. Happy now are the fishermen who love Him, and happy are the fishermen's children who love Him, and happy are all the little boys and girls who love Jesus. And they must all show their love by doing what Jesus tells them, and by trying to do something for Jesus.

This history may be found in Luke, v, 1-11.

'Up and doing little Christian,
    Up and doing while 'tis day;
Do the work the Master gives you,
    Do not loiter by the way:
For we all have work before us,
    You, dear child, as well as I.
Let us seek to learn our duty,
    And perform it cheerfully.'

C. F. R. P.

K

XX.

THE WIDOW AND HER SON.

WHEN a child dies, who is it sheds the most tears? Is it not the child's mother? If it be an only child who has died how very unhappy the mother is! And if that mother be a widow, she is the more to be pitied, because she has no husband to weep with her.

A long, long while ago a widow lost her only son. He was a young man. I do not know whether he was a good son or not, but I believe he was, for many people lamented for him at his death.

Soon after he died he was put in a coffin and carried by some men to be buried. The coffin had no lid — it was not like the coffins in this country, for they are screwed down.

The men were taking him out of the town where he had died into the country to be buried, and his mother walked near him crying very much, and a great many people followed.

They met on the road another crowd who were going towards the town. In that crowd there was a very wonderful man called the Lord Jesus Christ, the Son of God. He did such wonderful things that people followed Him about from place to place.

He saw the poor widow weeping. He knew all about her trouble without being told; He knew she had lost her only son, and He felt very sorry for her.

He came up to her, and said, 'Weep not.'

Jesus went up to the coffin where the young man was, and touched it. Immediately the men who carried it stood still. Then Jesus said, 'Young man, I say unto thee, Arise.'

The young man was dead. How could he get up out of his coffin?

But the dead hear the voice of Jesus, because He is God.

The young man sat up and began to speak. I wonder what he said. Did he praise God?

Do you think the widow left off weeping now? If she shed tears now, they must have been tears of joy. Jesus Himself gave the young man back to his mother.

Every one who saw this wonder was very much surprised and felt afraid. Many people said, 'A great prophet has risen up amongst us!'

They thought that God had sent Him. And so He had; the Father in heaven had sent His Son down into this world: and why? To die. Jesus came to die for sinners. Why did He give life to the young man? To show people that all He said was true.

He could make all dead people alive now, but He lets them lie in their graves till the day when He comes again. Then all that are in the graves shall hear His voice, and shall come forth. What a day that will be!

We often see a churchyard filled with graves. The ground is full of dead people, one lying above the other. What a sight it will be when all these dead people come up out of their graves!

Jesus will be there, seated upon a throne of glory, with all His bright angels round

Him. Then Jesus will judge the dead. He will say whether they shall go to heaven or hell.

Whom will He take to heaven? Those who believed that He died upon the cross to save them.

Whom will He cast into hell? Those who forget Him, and do not care for Him.

You may read the history of the widow's son in Luke, vii, 11–16.

'A widowed mother lost her son:
    She had no son beside,
He was her loved, her only one,
    And he fell sick and died.

And many a friend shed many a tear,
    But none had power to save;
They placed the body on a bier,
    To bear it to the grave.

When, lo! a company appears,
    A band by Jesus led:
Jesus can dry the mourner's tears,
    Jesus can raise the dead.

His heart, with tender pity moved,
    Felt for the widow's grief;
" Weep not," He said, and soon He proved
    His hand could give relief.

He touched the biei, — the mourners' eyes,
　Are fixed upon the Lord;
" Young man, I say to thee, Arise!"
　Is His almighty word.

He rises up — he speaks — he lives!
　No tear need now be shed,
Christ to the widowed mother gives
　The child she mourned as dead.'

D. A. T.

.' Within the churchyard, side by side,
　Are many long, low graves,
And some have stones set over them:
　On some the green grass waves.

Full many a little Christian child,
　Woman, and man, lie there;
And we pass by them every time
　When we go in to prayer.

But we believe a day shall come
　When all the dead shall rise;
When they who sleep down in the grave
　Will ope again their eyes.

For Christ our Lord was buried once;
　He died, and rose again;
He conquered death, He left the grave:
　And so will Christian men.'

MRS. C. F. ALEXANDER.

XXI.

THE WOMAN WHO WASHED THE SAVIOUR'S FEET.

WHEN the Lord Jesus Christ, the Son of God, lived in this world, some people hated Him, and some people loved Him. Do you think you should have loved Him? He was very kind, and gentle, and meek. You think you should have loved Him. But I must tell you something else about Him,—He hates sin; He has seen all the naughty things you have done. Should you love Him?

I will tell you the reason why some people loved Him, and why some people did not. It is this: people who were sorry for their sins loved Him,—people who were not sorry, did not.

There was a woman who had committed a great many sins. People thought her very bad. One day, when Jesus was sitting at dinner in a rich man's house, she went in, and she came behind Him, and she stood there crying.

What made her cry? It was her sins; she was sorry for having been very wicked.

Jesus was lying on a sofa at dinner, for it is the custom in some hot countries to lie down when you eat.

Jesus was not lying down quite flat; He was sitting up, resting on His elbow, but His feet were upon the sofa.

The poor woman began to wash His feet —not with water, not in a basin—but with her tears.

And how did she wipe them?

With her own long hair.

Then she kissed His feet, and poured sweet stuff called ointment on them.

The man who had invited Jesus to dine with him was called Simon: he was a proud man; he was angry when he saw the poor woman showing so much love to the Lord, and he thought in his heart, 'If Jesus were really as wise as people think, He would know what sort of a woman this is, and He would not let her touch Him'

Did Jesus know what sort of a woman she was? Oh, yes; He knew all the bad things she had ever done, and He had forgiven her —quite forgiven her.

Jesus saw into the woman's heart; He saw that she loved Him for having forgiven her. He saw into the heart of the proud Simon; He knew all he was thinking about,—so He asked him a question.

First, He told him a little history.

He said, 'There were two men who owed some money; one owed a great deal—the other a very little. A kind man to whom they owed the money said to both the men, "You need not pay me." Which would love the kind man the best—the man who owed much, or the man who owed little?'

Simon answered, 'The man who owed much will love the most.' Was that a right answer? Jesus said it was a right answer.

Why did Jesus ask Simon this question? To show why the woman loved Him so much.

She loved Him because she felt she had done a great many bad things, and that Jesus had forgiven all.

And why did not Simon love Him? Because he did not think he had done bad things; he thought he was very good. But he was not really good; he had behaved very rudely to the Lord.

It was the custom in that hot country always to bring water in a basin to wash the feet of your friends before they sat down to dinner; and it was the custom to kiss your friends when they came to see you, and to pour some sweet oil upon their heads. Simon had done none of these things to Jesus. But the woman had washed His feet with tears, and had kissed them, and had poured ointment on them.

And why did the woman love the Lord so much? Jesus told Simon the reason: 'Her sins, which are many, are forgiven.' That was the reason she loved the Lord so much.

Then Jesus said to the woman, 'Thy sins are forgiven.'

The men who sat at the table were angry when they heard those words; they thought that Jesus could not forgive sins; they did not believe that He was the Son of God; they did not know that His Father had sent Him down here to be nailed to a cross of wood, and to die for our sins.

Jesus did not answer those wicked men, but He spoke again to the woman. He said, 'Thy faith hath saved thee; go in peace.'

You may read this history in Luke, vii, 36, to the end.

> 'Just as I am — without one plea,
> But that Thy blood was shed for me,
> And that Thou bidd'st me come to Thee —
>   O Lamb of God, I come!
>
> Just as I am — and waiting not
> To rid my soul of one dark blot,
> To THEE — whose blood can cleanse each spot —
>   O Lamb of God, I come!
>
> Just as I am — Thou wilt receive,
> Wilt welcome, pardon, cleanse, relieve.
> Because Thy promise I believe,
>   O Lamb of God, I come!'
>   C. ELLIOTT.

XXII.

THE WILD MAN.

A LONG while ago there was a man whom the devils made very miserable. The devils were in him. This man would not wear any clothes; he would not live in a house, but he went to places where dead people were buried.

There were no churchyards in those days. Dead bodies were buried among the hills and rocks where no one lived. It was in those lonely places that this man liked to be.

Every one was afraid of passing near the place where he was, for he was very fierce. Sometimes people got hold of him, and put chains round his hands and feet: but he was so strong that he broke them and got away again, and then he cut his own flesh with sharp stones, so his body was covered with wounds and blood. It was dreadful to see him and to hear his cries.

No doctor could have made this man

well. But there was one person in the
world who could do everything,—Jesus, the
Son of God, was then living in the world.

It was a happy thing for that miserable
man that Jesus came near the place where
he was. He ran to Jesus, fell down at His
feet, and worshipped Him. Then Jesus
said, 'Come out of the man, thou unclean
spirit!' The man answered, 'What have
I to do with Thee, Jesus, Thou Son of the
Most High God? Art Thou come hither to
torment us before the time?'

It was the devils in the man who made
him speak, for they made the man do all
they pleased. These devils did not like to
be sent out of the man, and they begged
Jesus not to send them quite away, but to
let them go into a great herd of pigs that
were feeding among the hills close by; and
Jesus said, 'Go.'

As soon as the devils were in those poor
pigs, a very strange thing happened. The
pigs no longer fed quietly on the grass,
as they had done before, but they all ran
violently down a steep hill into the lake
which was at the bottom. And they were

choked in the deep water and died. In a few minutes two thousand pigs were destroyed.

There were some people who were paid to look after the pigs. When they saw that the poor beasts were all drowned, they were very much frightened, and ran into the town, and told their masters what had happened.

Soon there was a great crowd of people standing near Jesus, and there was one sitting at the feet of Jesus who looked gentle and harmless.

Who was that man? It was the same who had once been like a wild beast, fierce, and naked, and miserable. Now he was clothed, now he was quiet, now he was happy.

People remembered his face, and asked how he came to be so quiet. When they heard how Jesus had told the devils to come out of him, and how the devils had gone into the pigs and destroyed them, the people were frightened.

Why were they frightened? Ought they not to have been pleased? A man is worth more in God's sight than all the beasts in the world, because he has a soul, which beasts have not.

The foolish people begged Jesus to leave them. They were too sorry at having lost their pigs, and were afraid of losing other beasts. Was it not very selfish to care more for losing their pigs than for that poor man being made well? O yes—it was very selfish and very wicked.

Jesus would **not** stay with **them,** as they did not want Him. He had **come over the** water **in** a ship, and He got into a ship to go away.

But before He went — there was **a poor** man **who** asked to go with Him. You can guess who it was.

But Jesus said, 'Go home to thy friends, and tell them what great things the Lord hath done for thee.'

So the man went home, **and** told everybody in the town how Jesus had made him happy. I do not wonder that poor man wanted to be with the Lord Jesus, but it was better to stay behind and tell his friends about Him.

Would you like to be with Jesus? If you were to see Him, would you do as the poor man did? Would you wish to follow Jesus, or would you beg Jesus to go away? Ask the Lord Jesus now to come into your heart: say, 'Come, Lord Jesus.'

This history may be found in Matt. viii, 28, to the end; Mark, v, 1–20; Luke, viii, 26–40.

THE GIDDY LAMB.

'A giddy lamb, one afternoon,
 Strayed from its gentle brothers.
The tender shepherd missed it soon,
 Though he had many others.
It grieved him that a little one
 He used to love and cherish
Should wander helpless and alone
 In desert wilds to perish.

So night and day he went his way
 In sorrow, till he found it;
And when he saw it fainting lie,
 He clasped his arms around it:
And, closely sheltered in his breast,
 From every ill to save it,
He brought it to his home of rest,
 And pitied and forgave it.

Just so the Saviour will receive
   The little ones that fear Him;
Their pains remove, their sins forgive,
   And draw them gently near Him,—
Bless while they live, and when they die,
   And soul and body sever,
He'll bring them to His home on high,
   To dwell with Him for ever.'

           Falloon's Collection of Hymns.

THE DYING SAINT.

'Why do you weep?
   I am falling asleep,
And Jesus, my Shepherd,
   Is watching His sheep;
His arm is beneath me,
   His eye is above;
His Spirit within me
   Says, "Rest in My love:
With blood I have bought thee,
   And washed thee from sin:
With care I have brought thee
   My fold to be in:
Refreshed by still waters,
   In green pastures fed,
Thy day is gone by—
   I am making thy bed."'

           Extract in 'The Twin Brothers.

XXIII.

THE CHILD WHO DIED AND LIVED AGAIN.

ONE day a rich man came to Jesus, and fell down at His feet, and begged Him to come to his house. He said, ' My little daughter is dying.' He was very unhappy; he loved his little girl very much, and she was his only child. His name was Jairus, but I do not know the name of his little girl. But I *do* know her age—she was twelve years old. The father thought, that if Jesus only put His hands upon her He could make her well.

The Son of God was very kind to people in trouble. He went with the father, and He was followed by a great crowd. As He went along the road, He was pressed on every side by those who wanted to see Him, and to hear what He said.

Before He reached the rich man's house, some people came and said to the father, 'Your daughter is dead.' They told him

it was now useless for Jesus to come. They little knew what He could do: but Jesus said to the father, 'Do not be afraid, she shall be made well.'

When He came to the house, He only allowed three of His friends to come in with Him. Their names were Peter, James, and John.

There was a great noise and bustle in the house; there were men playing music, and people weeping and crying out with loud voices because the girl was dead.

When Jesus came into the room where she was lying, He said to these people, 'Why do you make this noise? The girl is not dead, she only sleeps.' Then they began to laugh at Him, for they knew the child was dead.

Why did Jesus say she slept? Because she was soon to be made alive. Her death was *like* sleep.

Jesus would not let the people who mocked stay in the room, but He let the girl's father and mother be there, and His own three friends. There were just these five in the room with Him when He went to the bed and took hold of the girl's hand, and said, 'Girl, I say unto thee, Arise.'

Immediately her spirit (or her soul) came again into her body. Then she was alive. She was now quite well; she was not weak now, as she had been; she got up out of her bed and walked about.

Then Jesus desired that something might be given her to eat.

Her parents were very much surprised. They had been afraid that Jesus would not be able to make her alive. They did not know He could do everything. They did not know that one day He will call all the dead people out of their graves.

I wonder whether that young girl loved Jesus. She was old enough to understand what He said. At twelve years old children can understand almost as well as men and women can.

Some children at twelve years old begin to think about their souls, and to say, 'What would become of me if I were to die?' Then some begin to pray and to say, 'Merciful

God, give me Thy Holy Spirit, for the sake of Jesus Christ.'

But there are some who at twelve years old will mind their parents no longer. They say, 'We are not little babies now, we will do as we please.' They forget all the kindness their parents have shown them for twelve years, and they forget the words that God has spoken, 'Honour thy father and thy mother.'

You can read the history of the daughter of Jairus in your Bible, in Mark, v, 23, 24, and 35, to end; Luke, viii, 41, 42, and 49, to end.

'The sun that lights the world shall fade,
    The stars shall pass away;
But I, a child immortal made,
    Shall witness their decay.

For I can never, never die,
    While God Himself remains,
But either live in heaven high,
    Or groan where darkness reigns.

If heaven and hell ne'er pass away,
    To Christ, oh! let me flee;
If pain be hard for one short day,
    What must FOR EVER be!'

Falloon's Collection

XXIV.

THE DANCING GIRL.

ONCE upon a time there was a little girl who could dance very well. Her name was Salome. Her parents were rich and great, but they did not fear God, and they had brought up their child in a wicked manner. Her uncle was a king. His name was Herod.

One day King Herod made a great supper to his lords and captains. It was his birthday, and this was the way in which he kept the day.

While the lords were eating and drinking and making merry,—in came a little girl. It was Salome who came in. She began to dance before the lords. Her uncle was much delighted with her dancing, and so were the lords. But, oh! what a bold child she was! She ought to have been ashamed to dance before all those gentlemen.

Her uncle Herod wished to reward her

for dancing, and **he said,** 'I will give you anything you like.'

What should you think Salome would wish to have? Some children would have asked for a doll, some **for a new** book, some would have asked to drive out, some to visit their cousins, and some would have **asked** for a holiday. But you could never **guess** what Salome asked for. She did not know herself **what to ask** for, but she ran to her mother **and told her** what the king had said.

Now, her mother **was** a very wicked woman—indeed, much more wicked than **King** Herod. Her name was Herodias. She soon told the little girl what to ask her uncle for.

There was a good man shut up in prison. **Why** had he been put in prison? He was not **a** thief or a murderer; he had done nothing wrong, but he had offended Herod. How? **He** had told the king of his wicked ways. The king in anger had shut him up, but he did not intend to kill this good man; he was afraid of doing that. Now, Herodias hated this holy man very much, and she said to her little girl, 'Ask the king to give you the head of John the Baptist in a great dish.' Oh, what a dreadful thing to ask for! I wonder the little girl could do it. It was right of her to ask her mother's advice, but when she heard her mother speak such wicked words, she ought to have said, 'Oh, mother, I cannot ask for that good man's head; let me rather ask that he may be let out of prison.'

But Salome was quite ready to do what her mother wished; she ran quickly back to the king and said, 'Give me the head of John the Baptist in a dish.'

The king was very sorry to hear this speech, but he thought to himself, 'I must keep my promise; I have said I would give Salome whatever she asked, and I must do it: if I do not, the lords sitting at the table will laugh at me.' What a foolish man Herod was! We ought not to keep a promise to do a wicked thing. It is better that men should laugh at us, than that God should be angry.

Herod immediately desired a man to go and cut off the head of John the Baptist. The man went with his sword and cut it off.

Do you think John was frightened when the man came with the sword to kill him? Oh, no; I am sure he was ready to die, for he knew that God had pardoned all his sins, and that He would take him to heaven

His head was placed in a dish, and given to the cruel child. She carried the dish to her mother. I do not know what that wicked woman did with the head. No doubt she was pleased to look upon it. and to think that the tongue that used to speak against sin could speak no longer. But she will not be pleased at the last day, when the Lord Jesus comes to judge the world.

What became of the body of John the Baptist? His friends came to the prison and asked for his body, and they took it and laid it in a grave, and then they went and told the Lord Jesus all about the death of John.　Jesus loved John very much, and He will make him happy for ever and ever.

You may read this history in your Bible, in Matt. xiv, 6–12; Mark, vi, 21–29.

THE VAIN GIRL.

'She has chosen the world,
　And its paltry crowd;
She has chosen the world,
　And an endless shroud;
She has chosen the world,
　With its misnamed pleasures;
She has chosen the world,
　Before heaven's own treasures.
Rev. ROBERT M'CHEYNE.

THE HAPPY CHILD.

I was a wandering sheep,
　I would not be controlled,
But now I love my Shepherd's voice,
　I love—I love the fold!

I was a wayward child;
　I once preferred to roam;
But now I love my Father's voice,
　I love—I love His home.'
BONAR.

XXV.

THE SUPPER ON THE GRASS.

IT is very pleasant to feed hungry people.
Teachers are very much pleased to see poor
children at a feast, drinking milk or tea,
and eating cake or bread and butter. They
like to see them sitting on the grass in
summer, and the kettle boiling on a fire of
sticks. Kind teachers like to hear their
little scholars singing thanks to God in
some sweet grace that they have learned.
This is a grace that I have heard children
sing:—

> ‘ Be present at our table, Lord;
> Be here and everywhere adored;
> These creatures bless, and grant that we
> May feast in Paradise with Thee.’

What creatures ? Bread and milk ? Yes,
they are God's creatures, for God created
them. You are His *living* creatures. I
hope you may live with Him in heaven in
Paradise.

The Son of God, when He lived in this world, fed a great many hungry people. These people had come from a great way off; they had left their cottages, and had walked over the green hills. Many of the mothers had brought their little children with them. All day long the people had been with Jesus. They liked to listen to Him; they stayed till it was getting dark, and till they were quite hungry. They had not brought enough food with them, and there were no houses or shops there. What could they do? They had a great way to go home, and the little children would be very much tired, and would be crying for their supper, and the mothers would not be able to carry them, and even the fathers would be quite weary.

Jesus was very kind. He pitied the poor people. He said to one of His friends, named Philip, 'Where shall we buy some bread?'

Philip was surprised that his Master should talk of buying bread for so many people, for there were more people than you

ever saw at church; there were enough to fill ten churches. But Jesus did not mean to *buy* bread for them; He had another plan in His mind.

His friends said to **Him**, 'Send these people into the villages near, that they may buy some bread for themselves.'

But Jesus said, 'No, they need not go away. How many loaves have we?'

One of His friends, named Andrew, said, 'We have only five loaves and two little fishes, but they are not nearly enough for so many people.'

You know, dear children, how soon five loaves are eaten up. A school of fifty children would soon get through five loaves.

But Jesus told His friends to make the people sit down on the grass.

Soon the green grass was covered with people sitting in rows, as children do at school, fifty men in every row. There were in all one hundred rows of men, besides women and children.

How many men were there?

Five thousand.

Then Jesus took the five loaves and the two fishes, and looked up to heaven and gave thanks to His Father, and brake the bread, and gave a piece to each of His friends, and a piece of the fishes. Then the twelve friends went to the men sitting on the grass, and gave some to each.

How much surprised everybody was to find that this little bread was enough for the suppers of all these people!—yes, and more than enough. This was the great wonder that Jesus did, for He is God, and can do everything.

The people could not eat all the bread. There was more than enough; a great deal was left lying upon the grass.

What was done with it?

Jesus would not let it be wasted: He told His friends to take some baskets and to gather up the bits of bread and fish. Twelve baskets were filled with these bits.

Everybody was astonished at this miracle. That evening they talked a great deal about Jesus, and said they felt sure that God had sent Him into the world.

Do you not think those little children loved Him who sat on the grass by the water-side, and who ate the bread that Jesus gave? Yes, I think they did.

And will not you love Him, too? You know that He died for you.

He is alive now. He is sitting in heaven on His Father's right hand; He knows whether you love Him; He gives you food every day; for it is He makes the rain to fall and the sun to shine upon the corn growing in the fields; He puts it into the hearts of rich people to give bread to little fatherless children.

But if you love Jesus you will try to please Him. Jesus calls the children who love Him His lambs, and, like a kind shepherd, He carries them in His arms.

Here is a verse out of the Bible about Jesus: 'He shall gather the lambs with His arm, and carry them in His bosom:' (Isa. xl, 11.)

You may read about the five loaves in four parts of the Testament: Matt. xiv,

15-21 ; Mark, vi, 35-44 ; Luke, ix, 12-17
John, vi, 3-14.

' And is it true, as I am told,
  That there are lambs within the fold
      Of God's beloved Son ?
  That Jesus Christ with tender care,
  Will in His arms most gently bear
      The helpless little one ?

Oh, yes ! I've heard my mother say
He never sent a child away,
    That scarce could speak or run ;
For when the parent's love besought
That He would touch the child she brought,
    He blessed the little one.

And I, a little straying lamb,
May come to Jesus as I am,
    Though goodness I have none ;
May now be folded in His breast,
As birds within the parent nest,
    And be His little one !

And He can do all this for me,
Because in sorrow on the tree
    He once for sinners hung ;
And having washed my sins away,
He now rejoices day by day,
    To cleanse the little one

                              A. M. Hall

XXVI.

CHRIST IN THE STORM.

THERE are a great many troubles in this life. Ask your father and your mother whether this is true. Your father will say. 'I have had a great many troubles : I have found it hard to get bread for my children.' Your mother will say, 'I have had a great deal of sorrow in bringing up my little family.'

My dear child, have you had any troubles? I am sure you have had some. Have you ever felt great pain? have you lost a little baby-brother or sister? have you got into disgrace? have you been punished for your faults?

There is one Friend to whom every one may go in every trouble. It is Jesus, the Son of God.

I will tell you how He helped some of His disciples out of trouble when He lived in this world.

One evening they went into a ship. Jesus did not go with them; He stayed where He was, and spent the night all alone on the top of a mountain, praying to His Father, God.

The disciples were in their little ship on the water when the wind began to blow very hard indeed. The waves rose high, and the ship was tossed about. Every moment the poor men were afraid that the water would fill their ship, and that they should sink to the bottom of the sea.

All night long the disciples were in sad distress, trying with all their might to row their ship to land, but all they could do was of no use.

At last they saw a man walking on the sea. There He was in the midst of the great waves, walking as on the dry land He went faster than the ship, and seemed as if He would pass by it.

The disciples did not know who it was. They thought it could not be a man with a body like ours; they supposed it was a

A.EVANS.

spirit, who has no body. They were **very** much frightened, and they cried **out in** their trouble.

Then they heard **a voice saying**, 'It is I; be not afraid.'

Whose voice was that?

You know, and they knew; it was **the** voice of Jesus. Though the winds were whistling and the waves roaring, **His** voice could be heard.

One of the disciples, named Peter, said, 'Lord, if it be Thou, bid **me** come untc Thee on the water.'

Jesus said, 'Come.'

So Peter got out of the ship and **walked** on the water to go to Jesus. He believed **that** Jesus could help him to walk on the water, and Jesus did help him.

But when Peter saw how high the wind was he began to be afraid.

This was wrong. He ought to have trusted in **Jesus.**

Soon he felt **that** he was sinking, and he cried out, 'Lord, save me.'

Jesus heard that short prayer; He was

very near, and He stretched out His hand, and caught hold of Peter.

Trusting in God is called faith. Peter had a little faith, but not much. So he was able to walk on the water a little way, but not far.

Jesus went into the ship and took Peter with Him, and as soon as He was there the wind left off blowing. Then all the disciples came round Him and worshipped Him, saying 'Truly Thou art the Son of God.'

It is this Jesus who can help you in your troubles. Will you trust Him? Do not be like Peter, and only trust Him a little while; but go on trusting in Him, and you will find that He will keep you safe, and make you happy. He forgives sins, which no one else can do, because He died upon the cross to save us from our sins. When we are dying He will not leave us if we trust in Him, but He will comfort us and take us to heaven.

This history you will find in Matt. xiv 22–33; Mark. vi, 45–52.

'A little ship was on the sea,
  It was a pretty sight;
It sailed along so pleasantly,
  And all was calm and bright.

When lo! a storm began to rise,
  The wind grew loud and strong;
It blew the clouds across the skies,
  It blew the waves along.

And all but ONE were sore afraid
  Of sinking in the deep:
His head was on a pillow laid,
  And He was fast asleep.

"Master, we perish! Master, save!"
  They cried—their Master heard:
He rose—rebuked the wind and wave,
  And stilled them with a word.

He to the storm says, "Peace—be still,"
  The raging billows cease;
The mighty wind obeys His will,
  And all are hushed to peace.

Oh! well we know it was the Lord,
  Our Saviour and our Friend;
Whose care of those who trust His word
  Will *never*—never end.'

D. A. T.

XXVII.

THE PRAYING MOTHER.

Can we pray too much? No, we cannot. God likes to hear us pray; He is never tired of listening to us. Is He not kind? Men are soon tired of hearing beggars ask for money; but men are not like God.

When Jesus, the Son of God, was in this world, there was a poor woman who longed very much to see Him. I do not think she had ever seen Him, but she had heard of Him. She had been brought up to worship idols; she did not belong to the people of Israel, who worshipped the true God. No, she was a poor heathen; but Jesus cares for the poor heathen, and He cared for this poor woman.

She had a little girl very ill at home. A wicked spirit, called a devil, tormented her. The mother knew that Jesus could make her little daughter well, so she went to look for Him.

When the poor woman saw Jesus she cried out, 'Have mercy on me, O Lord, Thou Son of David, my daughter is grievously vexed with a devil.' Why did she call Jesus the Son of David! David was a great king, who had long been dead, and Jesus was one of his great-great-grandchildren. Jesus liked to hear people call Him the Son of David, for it showed they believed in the promise God made to David.

What promise?

That he should have a son who should be a great king.

Jesus was this great king.

What did He say to this poor woman, when she seemed so unhappy?

He said nothing at all; so she went on crying out for mercy.

The disciples did not like to hear the poor woman crying out, 'Have mercy on me.' As they walked along with Jesus, the poor woman followed them with her cries. So the disciples went to Jesus and said, 'Send her away, for she crieth after us,'

But Jesus did not send her away, though at first He seemed unkind, for He said, 'I am only sent to the lost sheep of the house of Israel.' This poor woman was not an Israelite.

Did she go away when she heard Jesus speak in this way? No, she did not; she came nearer than before: she fell at His feet and worshipped Him, saying, 'Lord, help me.'

What a short prayer—only three words! but it came from the heart; it was such a prayer, as God likes to hear.

Yet Jesus still seemed unkind, for He said, 'It is not fit to take the bread from the children, and to throw it to dogs.'

Did He mean that this poor woman was a dog, and that the people of Israel were His children?

Oh, no; He did not really think this woman was a dog! He only spoke so, that she might go on praying.

She made a very sweet answer this time. She said, 'The dogs under the table eat of the children's crumbs.'

Was not that a meek answer, and a wise answer? She did not say she was not a dog; she meant to say, 'If I am a dog, may I not have crumbs? Though you love the people of Israel best, yet you will have pity on a poor heathen like me.' This is what she meant to say.

Jesus kept her waiting no longer. He said to her, 'O woman, great is thy faith; go thy way, the devil is gone out of thy daughter.'

So the woman went home, and found her daughter lying on the bed. The devil had left the girl at the very moment when Jesus spoke. Then the girl grew quiet and easy, but it seems she was weak and tired, and wanted rest.

Could the mother ever forget what Jesus had said? 'O woman, great is thy faith!' Jesus had praised her. Why was He so much pleased with her? Because she believed that He could do everything, and that He loved her, and was ready to help her.

Jesus likes us to believe that He is as

kind as He is great. Whatever happens, we
ought always to think, 'Jesus is kind.' Did
He not die for us on the cross? Does He
wish to hurt us?

You may read this history of the praying mother in Matt. xv, 21-28; Mark, vii,
24-30.

' Who are they whose little feet,
   Pacing life's dark journey through,
Now have reached that heavenly seat
   They have ever kept in view?

"I from Greenland's frozen land,"
   " I from India's sultry plain,"
"I from Afric's barren sand,"
   " I from islands of the main!"

" All our earthly journey past,
   Every tear and pain gone by,
Here together met at last
   At the portal of the sky."

Each the welcome " Come!" awaits
   Conquerors over death and sin.
Lift your heads, ye golden gates!
   Let the little travellers in!'

                JAMES EDMESTON

XXVIII.

CHRIST SHINING ON THE MOUNTAIN.

Did you ever think how the Lord Jesus looked when He was walking about this world? There is no picture of Him to be seen, but we are told in the Bible that He looked like other men. He was not bright as angels are, neither did He wear fine clothes as princes do. If you had seen Him, you would have taken Him for a poor man. You could not have told by His look that He was the Son of God.

But once He let His friends see a wonderful change in Him. He took three of His disciples to the top of a mountain; their names were Peter, James, and John. When Jesus wished to be in a quiet place, He often went to a mountain, because it is not easy to climb up high places, so that it is very seldom that people come there.

Why did Jesus wish to find a quiet place?

Because He was going to pray to His Father in heaven.

He spent the night on that mountain. During the night He prayed. While He was praying, the disciples saw a great change in Him. In the midst of the darkness they saw His face shine like the sun, and His clothes became as white as snow, and as bright as the light. There were never any clothes seen on earth so white and shining.

Two men were with Jesus. Where had they come from? From heaven. They were two men who had lived upon the earth a long while ago, and who had been taken to heaven, and now they were come down to talk to the Lord Jesus. One of these men was named Moses; he had once died, and God had buried him. The other man was Elijah; he had never died, but had gone to heaven in a chariot of fire: he had been carried by bright angels into heaven.

And what were these men talking about? They were speaking about a very sad and

sorrowful thing that would soon happen —
about Jesus being nailed to the cross of
wood for our sins. How sweet it must be to
listen to heavenly men, and to hear them talk
to the Son of God! I do not wonder that
the disciples were pleased.

At last it seemed as if these men, all
bright and glorious, were going back tc
heaven. Then Peter said, 'Lord, it is good
for us to be here : let us make three tents ;
one for Thee, one for Moses, and one for
Elijah.'

Peter wanted to have these heavenly men
always with him, but they could not stay
down here. Peter did not know what he
said, for he was very much afraid.

While he was speaking, a bright cloud
came and covered Jesus and those two bright
ones. The disciples were frightened at the
sight.

A voice came out of the cloud, saying,
'This is My beloved Son, in whom I am well
pleased : hear ye Him.'

Whose voice was that ? It was the voice
of God the Father.

The disciples were afraid when they heard it, and they fell upon their faces. They could not look at the brightness of that cloud, for God was there; but the great God did not hurt them. He did not punish them for their sins. No; He only commanded them to hear His beloved Son. He sent His Son into the world to save us, and if we believe in Jesus we shall be saved.

I do not know how long the disciples remained with their faces on the ground, but they did not dare to look up till they felt some one touch them, and heard a gentle voice, 'Arise, and be not afraid.'

Whose touch was that? Whose gentle voice?

When the disciples looked up they saw Jesus, but the bright cloud shone there no longer. The disciples looked round about, but they could not see the two heavenly men; there was no one but Jesus. They were not afraid to be alone with Him, for they knew Him well, and loved Him too. They walked down the mountain with Him.

Could they ever forget the glorious sight

they had seen at the top? They could not, but Jesus said to them as they walked, 'Tell no man what you have seen till the Son of man be risen again from the dead.' Jesus called Himself the Son of man.

The disciples did not know He would soon be buried in a grave, and that He would rise again in three days. But they minded what Jesus said, and told no one about the brightness on the mountain till after Jesus had been crucified and had come to life again. Then they told people all that you have now heard. Is it not a very wonderful history?

Jesus is now shining as bright in heaven as He shone on that mountain. When you see Him coming in the clouds He will look very glorious. Good men, who lived a long while ago, will come with Him. And if you love Jesus you shall stay with Him for ever. Oh, how happy you will be!

You may read the history of Christ on the mountain in Matt. xvii, 1–9 ; Mark, ix, 2–10 ; Luke, ix, 28–36.

' Here we suffer grief and pain,
Here we meet to part again :
In heaven we part no more.
    Oh, that will be joyful!
    Joyful, joyful, joyful!
    Oh, that will be joyful,
When we meet to part no more!

All who love the Lord below,
When they die to heaven will go,
And sing with saints above.
    Oh, that will be joyful!
    Joyful, joyful, joyful!
    Oh, that will be joyful,
When we meet to part no more!

Holy children will be there,
Who have sought the Lord by prayer,
From every Sunday-school.
    Oh, that will be joyful!
    Joyful, joyful, joyful!
    Oh, that will be joyful!
When we meet to part no more!

Oh, how happy we shall be!
For our Saviour we shall see,
Exalted on His throne!
    Oh, that will be joyful!
    Joyful, joyful, joyful!
    Oh, that will be joyful.
When we meet to part no more. .

XXIX.

THE MISERABLE BOY.

THERE is a wicked creature called Satan, or the devil; he has not a body, as you have, but he can think—he thinks of doing wicked things; he hates God, and he hates everybody; he hates you, my little boy and my little girl,—he would like to make you unhappy: he is very unhappy himself, and he tries to make us unhappy too. There are a great many devils, and they help one another to do harm.

I am now going to tell you of a poor little boy who was made very wretched by one of the devils. It seemed as if this boy was mad. A wicked spirit was in him, and tormented him. This spirit was deaf and dumb. Sometimes it would tear the boy, and make him cry out with pain, and foam at the mouth, and gnash his teeth, and fall on the ground. Sometimes this poor child would rush into the water to drown himself, and sometimes into the fire to burn himself. His father loved him, and could not bear to see him in this dreadful state. But his father could not cure him, nor could any doctor.

At last this poor father heard of Jesus Christ, the Son of God, who came down from heaven to save us from Satan and all the devils. The father of the boy thought, ' I will take my dear son to Jesus, and ask Him to cure him.'

But when the father came to the place where he expected to find Jesus, he did not find Him ; he found only His disciples,— and not all of them — only nine.

Where was Jesus ? He was gone away for a little while, to pray to God His Father in heaven, upon the top of a hill.

What could the poor man do now ? Could the disciples help his boy ? He begged them to try. Jesus had once told them that they should be able to cast out devils ; so they tried to cast the devil out of this boy, but they could not. A great crowd of people gathered round the boy

and the disciples, and some wise men were
there, called scribes ; these scribes did not
love Jesus, and they were always glad when
the disciples could not do wonderful things.

No one knew how soon Jesus would come
back. He had gone away the day before,
and now it was morning. At last the people
saw Him coming, and they ran to meet
Him. Three of His disciples were with Him
—Peter, James, and John. How glad the
poor father must have been to see Jesus!
He fell on his knees and said, 'Lord, I pray
you, have mercy on my son, for he is my
only child.' And then he told Him all
about the boy.

Jesus said, ' Bring thy son here to Me.'

But as the boy was coming, the devil
threw him on the ground, and there the
poor creature lay foaming at the mouth.
Ah! that devil knew who Jesus was. All
the devils know the Son of God, and are
afraid of Him.

The poor man was very unhappy to
see his son lying in such pain upon the
ground, and he said to Jesus, ' If Thou

canst do anything, have pity upon us and help us.'

If the father had known Jesus better, he would not have said, '*If* Thou canst;' he would have felt quite sure that Jesus could cure him.

Then Jesus asked the man if he believed.

What could the poor father say? He did believe a little, but he did not believe as much as he ought.

Immediately the man cried out, 'Lord, I believe: help Thou mine unbelief.' As he said this, the tears came into his eyes. Poor man! It was a good prayer he made when he said to Jesus, 'Help Thou mine unbelief.' It showed that he believed that Jesus was God, for who but God can make people believe?

While the Lord was talking with the father, more people came running to the place—soon there would have been too great a crowd.

Then Jesus said to the devil, 'Thou dumb and deaf spirit, I command thee come out of him, and enter no more into him.'

This deaf spirit heard the words of Jesus, this dumb spirit was able to cry out; it tore the boy, and came out of him.

The people looked at the boy and said, 'He is dead.' There he was lying on the ground, and looking just like a dead person.

Jesus went to him, took his hand, and lifted him up. The child was alive and quite well. Jesus gave him to his father.

How happy that father must have been! Did he now believe in Jesus? He knew now that Jesus could cure his child.

Afterwards the disciples went into a house with their dear Master, and they said, 'Why could not we cast out the devil?' Jesus said, 'Because of your unbelief.'

The disciples had not prayed as much as they ought, and so they did not believe as much as they ought. Jesus had given them the power to do wonders, but they could not do them except when they believed in the Son of God.

Jesus can still do everything. He sits at His Father's right hand, and He hears the prayers of men in this world. In all

your troubles go to Him.   Say, 'Lord, help
mine unbelief.'   He is very kind, and pities
people in distress.

You may read this history in Matt. xvii,
14–21; Mark, ix, 14–29; Luke, ix, 37–42.

'Jesus, Saviour, pity me!
 Hear me when I cry to Thee!
 I've a very naughty heart,
 Full of sin in every part:
 I can never make it good,
'Wash me, wash me in Thy blood.
　Jesus, Saviour, pity me!
　Hear me, when I cry to Thee.

Short has been my pilgrim way,
Yet I'm sinning every day:
Though I am so young and weak,
Lately taught to run and speak,
Yet in evil I am strong,
Far from Thee I've lived too long.
　Jesus, Saviour, pity me!
　Hear me when I cry to Thee.

Though I cannot cease from guilt,
Thou canst cleanse me, and Thou wilt,
Since Thy blood for sin was shed,
Crowned with thorns Thy blessed head
Thou, who loved and suffered so,
Ne'er wilt bid me from Thee go.
　Jesus, Thou wilt pity me!
　Save me when I cry to Thee.'
                    Dublin Farthing Hymn Book.

XXX.

THE TWO SISTERS; OR, MARTHA AND MARY.

A LONG while ago there lived two women, named Martha and Mary. They were sisters, and they lived in a house in a pretty village, on the side of a green hill. Its name was Bethany. I cannot tell what kind of a house Martha and Mary lived in —whether it was a large house or only a cottage.

One day a visitor came to their house; it was such a visitor as never came to your father's house. Perhaps good ministers come sometimes to see your father. But such a minister never came to your father's house as came to Martha's house. He was better than any minister—greater than any king—more glorious than any angel—and yet He was a very poor man. He had no carriage to ride in; He had no horse nor even an ass; He had no servants, and no

house of His own. He might have been
rich, but He chose to be poor; He walked
about and talked to the people that He saw
in the road, and told them about God His
Father in heaven. Sometimes He came
into people's houses and rested Himself.
Kind people gave Him food to eat.

Martha used to beg Jesus to come into
her house, and Mary was very glad to see
Him enter.

When Jesus was come in, He began to
speak about God His Father, and about
heaven. Should you have liked to hear what
He said? Mary sat down at His feet, and
listened to every word. People in that
country often sat upon the floor, or on a low
stool. Mary liked to sit near Jesus, where
she could hear Him.

But where was Martha? She was gone
to get ready the dinner. She wished to
make a very fine dinner for the Lord
Jesus.

But did Jesus care about eating nice
things? Oh, no; He wanted very little.
Martha could easily have brought Him a

piece of bread or fish, or a honeycomb, and then she might have sat down with Mary and listened to the Lord. But instead of doing this, she was vexed because Mary did not help her to get ready the dinner; and she came into the room where Mary was sitting so happy, and she said to the Lord, 'Do you not care that my sister has left me to do all the work alone? Will you not tell her to help me?'

Are not you sorry she said this?

Mary did not answer, but Jesus did; 'Martha, Martha, you trouble yourself about a great many things. There is only one thing that we cannot do without, and Mary has chosen that good thing, and it shall not be taken away from her.'

What was the good thing Mary had chosen? Was it not to hear about God and heaven? It is better to know about God than to have all the things in the world. If you had a fine house fit for a king, and a hundred servants to wait upon you, and a carriage with six horses to draw it, yet some day you must leave them all,

for some day you must die. But if you
knew about God, and if He had forgiven
you all your sins, then when you died you
would be as happy as the angels, and sing
sweet hymns to a golden harp.

I wonder what Martha did after Jesus
ad spoken to her; I hope she sat down to
listen. She was a good woman and loved
Jesus, and I know she is with Him in
neaven now.

Do you like to hear the words of Jesus?
You can read them in the New Testament;
they are written down there, and they are
such sweet words. Is not this a sweet
verse, 'The Son of man is come to seek and
to save them which are lost?' And is not
this sweet, 'Him that cometh unto Me I
will in no wise cast out?'

There is no harm in liking to play, for
you are a child; but if you love Jesus you
will like to think of His words, and sometimes you will pray to Him, and say, 'Forgive my sins, O blessed Jesus. Make me
good; give me Thy Holy Spirit; take me to
heaven when I die.'

You may read the history of Martha and Mary in Luke, x, 38, to the end.

The words of Jesus to Martha .

'Mary hath chosen that good part which shall not be taken away from her.'

'Suffer me to come to Jesus,
   Parents dear, forbid me not;
By His blood from hell He frees us,
   Makes us fair without a spot.

Suffer me to run unto Him;
   Gentle sisters, come with me:
Oh, that all I love but knew Him!
   Then my heaven a home would be.

Loving playmates, gay and smiling,
   Bid me not forsake the cross;
Hard to bear is your reviling,
   Yet for Jesus all is dross.

Yes, though all the world have chid me,
   Father, mother, sister, friend,
Jesus never will forbid me!
   Jesus loves me to the end!

REV. ROBERT M'CHEYNE.

XXXI.

THE CRIPPLE.

SOMETIMES, as we walk along, we meet a
man with only one eye, or one arm, or one
leg, or who has a hump-back. How ought
we to feel when we see them? We ought
to pity them; we ought to think to ourselves, 'How painful it must be to limp
along, instead of walking easily!' Then
we ought to thank God for His kindness to
us in giving us so many limbs, and keeping
us from being hurt. If our mothers had
dropped us out of their arms when we
were babies, our backs might have been
broken. If a playfellow had put a stick
into one of our eyes, we might have lost
our precious sight.

When Jesus the Son of God lived in this
world, He took great notice of poor cripples.
Once when He was in a place like a church,
called a synagogue, He saw a woman who
was bent double. She could not lift herself

P

up to look at Him, but He saw her. I
wonder how she got to the synagogue.
Perhaps she lived very near, or perhaps her
friends helped her to come, or perhaps she
crept along by herself.

How glad she must have been that she
had come there when she heard Jesus
teaching! There never was such a teacher
as He was. He spoke so gently and so
sweetly that poor people liked to listen to
Him, and to hear Him say, 'Come unto Me,
all ye that are weary and heavy laden, and
I will give you rest.'

Jesus saw the poor cripple, and He called
her to Him. The people who stood round
heard Him call, and they watched to see
what He did. First Jesus said to her,
'Woman, thou art loosed from thy infirmity.'
What was her infirmity? It was being
bent double. Then He laid His hands
on her, and immediately she was made
straight.

What a sight it was to see that woman
lift herself up and all at once become as
straight as other women!

What did she do when she was made straight? She began to praise God. This woman loved God. It was the devil who had bent her back double. God sometimes allows the devil to hurt the bodies of good people, but He does not let the devil have their souls.

This poor woman had been bent double eighteen years, yet she had gone on loving God, and now at last she was saved out of her trouble. Do you think that everybody was glad to see her made straight? Oh, no; there were some wicked people there, who hated Jesus, and they could not bear to see Him do wonders, because they were afraid more people would believe that He was the Son of God.

The chief man in the synagogue was wicked; it was he who used to offer up the prayers to God, yet his heart was full of malice and envy. After he had seen Jesus make the woman straight—he was very angry, and he said to the people, 'Do not come here on the Sabbath-day to be made well, but come on one of the six weekdays.' But the people had not come to the synagogue only to be made well, they had come to be taught.

Jesus Himself answered the wicked man; He called him by a dreadful name — 'Hypocrite!' He can see into the heart, and He knows who pretend to be good when they are really wicked; those people are hypocrites.

What did Jesus say to the hypocrite? He said, 'Does not every one here loose his ox or his ass from the stall on the Sabbath-day, and lead him to drink water? And ought not this woman, whom the devil has bound eighteen years, to be loosed on the Sabbath-day?' What could the hypocrite answer to this question? No one could answer it. It was plain that if an ass ought to be kindly treated on the Sabbath, a poor woman who trusted in God ought to be made happy on the Sabbath. This woman did trust in God, and Jesus called her a daughter of Abraham. Abraham trusted in God, and she was like him.

Perhaps some poor cripple will read this

story. Be comforted, God cares for you. He could make you straight and strong. He has some wise reason for letting you be crooked. He gave His only Son to die for your sins upon the cross; He knows whether you love Him. At the last day all the people who have been buried will rise out of their graves with new bodies. Cripples who have loved God will then be bright and beautiful, like the Son of God.

Children who are tall, and straight, and strong, you should love God for making you so. You can show your love to Him by being very kind and gentle to all who are lame, and weak, and sick, and sad. Perhaps you can do something to comfort them, though you cannot heal them as Jesus did.

You will find the history of this poor woman in Luke, xiii, 10–17.

‘ Jesus is our Shepherd, wiping every tear ;
Folded in His bosom, what have we to fear ?
Only let us follow whither He doth lead,
To the thirsty desert, or the dewy mead.

Jesus is our Shepherd; well we know His voice;
How its gentlest whisper makes our heart rejoice!
Even when it chideth, tender is its tone;
None but He shall guide us; we are His alone.

Jesus is our Shepherd; for the sheep He bled;
Every lamb is sprinkled with the blood He shed:
Then on each He setteth His own secret sign,—
"They that have My Spirit, THESE," saith He, "are
    MINE."

H. STOWELL.

   'I heard the voice of Jesus say,
     "Come unto Me and rest;
    Lay down, thou weary one, lay down
     Thy head upon my breast."

    I came to Jesus as I was—
     Weary, and worn, and sad;
    I found in Him a resting-place,
     And He has made me glad.'

BONAR.

XXXII.

THE BLIND BEGGAR OF JERUSALEM.

A LONG while ago there was a blind beggar in Jerusalem. He was a young man, but he could not work because of his blindness —so he begged.

One day some men passed by; one of these men was the Son of God. He was come down from heaven to live in this world for a little while. Why did He come down? It was to save us sinners from going to hell. He saw this blind beggar, and He told His friends that He would cure him.

You will be surprised to hear the strange manner in which He cured him. He made a plaster of the dust of the ground by wetting it with His spittle, and then He put it on the blind man's eves. You would have thought that by this way his eyes would be made worse.

Then Jesus told the beggar to go and wash in a pool, or pond, a little way off.

The beggar went and washed, for he could find his way about Jerusalem, as he had lived there a long while. When he had washed he found he could see.

Everybody was very much surprised to see him walking along the streets with his eyes open. Some people wondered whether it was the same man who once sat and begged. Other people were sure it was the same man, and other people thought it could not be the same, but only a man very much like the blind beggar.

But when he heard what people said, he answered them, 'I am the same man.'

Then the people said, 'How were your eyes opened?'

Then he told them that a man named Jesus had cured him. He did not know who Jesus was, and he had never seen Him, but he knew that He had been very kind to him, and had done a great wonder in giving him sight.

Though Jesus was so very good, yet many people in Jerusalem did not love Him. They hated Him because He told them of their sins; so they were very angry with the blind man for saying that Jesus had cured him. They said to him, 'It was not Jesus who made you see, it was God—praise Him; Jesus is a wicked man.'

The blind man did not know that Jesus was God as well as man, but he was sure that He was good, and he said so.

This made the wicked men more angry than before, and at last they said they would have no more to do with him, and that they would not speak to him, or take any notice of him. Was not this very cruel?

Jesus knew that the poor blind beggar was ill-treated, and He went to him. Jesus could easily find him, for He is God, and sees everybody by day and by night. I do not know where the poor man was when Jesus found Him—whether he was in the house, or in the street, or in the temple

When the man saw Jesus, he did not know who He was, for he had never seen Him before. But he had heard His voice and perhaps he knew that voice again.

Jesus said to him, 'Do you believe on the Son of God?'

The man answered, 'Who is He, Lord, that I might believe on Him?'

Then said Jesus, 'You have seen Him, and He is now talking with you.'

Then the man said, 'Lord, I believe,' and he worshipped Him.

I do not know what happened afterwards to that blind man, but I am sure he is happy now in heaven, for he believed in Jesus, the Son of God.

Everybody will be happy who believes in Jesus, as this blind man did. If Jesus were to say to you, 'Do you believe on the Son of God?' could you say, 'Lord, I believe?'

If you believe in Jesus, then you love Him, and you will try to please Him. If wicked boys and girls laugh at you because you wish to please God, do not mind what they say. Jesus hears them when they laugh at you, and He will make you happy.

You may read this history in the ninth

chapter of the Gospel according to St. John.

' Jesus, who lives beyond the sky,
Came down to be a man, and die;
And in the Bible we may see
How very good He used to be.

He went about, He was so kind,
To cure poor people who were blind,
And many who were sick and lame,
He pitied them, and did the same.

And more than that—He told them, too,
The things which God would have them do;
And was so gentle and so mild,
He would have listened to a child.

But such a cruel death He died—
He was hung up and crucified!
And those kind hands that did such good,
They nailed them to a cross of wood.

And so He died!   And this is why
He came to be a man and die!
The Bible says he came from heaven,
That we might have our sins forgiven.

He knew how wicked men had been,
And knew that God must punish sin;
So out of pity Jesus said,
He'd bear the punishment instead.

JANE TAYLOR.

LITTLE CHILDREN.

SOME people are **very** fond of children. Other people think them troublesome, take no notice of them, **or** speak roughly to them. When Jesus, the Son of God, **was** in this world, He was very kind to children, and **now** He lives in heaven He loves them still.

Once when He **was** in a house, He called a little child, and took **him in His arms.**

And why?

There **were** some men in the house **who** had been disputing together.

What had they been disputing about?

Who should be the greatest?

It is proud to wish to be great. A little child does not wish to be great; it likes better to be with its own mother than to go in a carriage with the Queen.

Jesus showed this little child to the men who wished to be great. He set him in

the midst of them, and said, 'Except you
become as little children, you shall not
enter into the kingdom of heaven. If any
one shall humble himself as this little
child, he is greatest in the kingdom of
heaven.'

You see that Jesus loves humble, meek,
gentle people, who are like lambs and
doves. Here is a prayer for a little child :—

'Gentle Jesus, meek and mild,
Look upon a little child ;
Pity my simplicity,
Suffer me to come to Thee.'

There were some other little children
whom Jesus took in His arms. Their
mothers brought them to the Lord.

Should you have liked to see those
mothers, with their little darlings in their
arms, coming to Jesus?

When they came, those men were there
who once disputed who should be the
greatest. I mean the disciples ; they were
good men, but not nearly as good as Jesus
was. They did not like to see the mothers
bringing little children in their arms ; they

Q

thought the children would be troublesome, and they told the mothers to take them away. How sorry those poor women would have been to take their little ones back again! for they wanted Jesus to touch them, to pray for them, and to bless them. But Jesus heard the disciples speak unkindly to the women, and He was much displeased, and He said to the disciples, 'Let the little children come to Me: do not tell them to go away; for of such is the kingdom of heaven.' Then He took the dear little creatures in His arms, put His hands upon them, and blessed them.

Every good mother wishes to bring her little children to Jesus. She cannot carry them in her arms now, as those mothers did; but she can talk to them about Jesus, and teach them to fold their little hands in prayer; and she can go and pray to Jesus for them.

Here is a hymn that a fond mother wrote on purpose for her own child :—

When children came the Saviour nigh,
  And those around forbade them,
" Forbid them not, " was His reply,
  And on his breast He laid them :
He took them in His arms of love,
  With sacred kiss He press'd them,
And to His Father's throne above,
  His prayer ascending, bless'd them.

' And thou, my darling cherub child,
  While fondly I caress thee,
I pray that, as on *them* he smil'd,
  His smile of love may bless thee ;
And when by thine ascending wing
  This world shall be forsaken,
Thy spirit may to Jesus spring,
  And to His breast be taken.'

Christian Melodies.

Another time Jesus was pleased by hearing some children praising Him. Jesus was in that beautiful house called the Temple, when these children came in. They saw the wonderful things He did; they saw Him make blind people see, and lame people walk, and they cried out, 'Hosannah to the Son of David!' This was a prayer. The word 'Hosannah' means, 'Save, Lord, we beseech Thee.' The children called

Jesus the Son of David. David was a great king. But Jesus was the Son of a greater king than David—He was the Son of God.

Did He like to hear the children praising Him? Yes, He did; but there were some wicked men there who did not like to hear them. They said to Him, 'Do you hear what these children say?' And Jesus said, 'Yes. Have you never read, Out of the mouths of babes and sucklings thou hast perfected praise?' Those words are in the eighth psalm of David. It is a dreadful thing to hear a child use wicked words, but it is very sweet to hear him praise God —it makes one think of the angels in heaven.

You may read about Christ and the children in Matt. xix, 13–15; xxi, 15, 16, Mark, ix, 33–37; x, 13–16. Luke, xviii, 15–17.

' " The Master has come over Jordan,"
　　Said Hannah the mother one day;
" He is healing the people who throng Him,
　　With a touch of His finger, they say;

And now I shall carry the children,
  Little Rachel, and Samuel, and John,
I shall carry the baby, Esther,
  For the Lord to look upon."

So over the hills of Judah,
  Along by the vine-rows green,
With Esther asleep on her bosom,
  And Rachel her brothers between ;

'Mong the people who hung on His teaching,
  Or waited His touch and His word,
Through the row of proud Pharisees listening,
  She press'd to the feet of the Lord.

" Now why shouldst thou hinder the Master,'
  Said Peter, " with children like these ?
See how, from the morning till evening,
  He teacheth and healeth disease."

Then Christ said, " Forbid not the children ;
  Permit them to come unto Me ; "
And He took in His arms little Esther,
  And Rachel He set on His knee ;

And the heavy heart of the mother
  Was lifted all earth care above,
As He laid His hands on the brothers,
  And bless'd them with tenderest love.'

JULIA GILL.

XXXIV.

THE TEN SICK MEN.

It is very common to meet sick people in the streets, but did you ever see ten sick people all standing together? I think not.

Yet once ten very sick people were seen together. They were called lepers. What is a leper? It is a man whose skin is covered with white sores breaking out, and whose flesh is beginning to crumble away. Sometimes the ends of his fingers drop off, and then his hands or his feet, till only the stumps are left. It would make you sad to see one of these poor lepers. But, oh, how very sad it must have been to see ten lepers standing together!

I will tell you why they all kept together. It was because they were not allowed to be with people who were well—not even to touch them; so what could the poor creatures do? They did not like always to be alone, and they were glad to keep company with each other. They were not allowed to walk in

the streets of a town, lest they should touch
the people who were passing by; they were
obliged to be in the country amongst the
trees and the fields.   It is pleasant to be in
the country — yes, very pleasant for people
who are well, but it was not pleasant for the
poor lepers; no place was pleasant for them.

One day, as the ten lepers were all
together, they saw a man coming along the
way, and going towards a village. They
knew who this man was; they must have
seen Him before. They knew He was Jesus.

The ten lepers had heard of Jesus, and
when they saw Him passing by they called
out very loud, 'Jesus, Master, have mercy
on us!' They did not dare to come near
Him, but they hoped He would hear their
voices.

And He did hear them, and said, 'Go,
show yourselves to the priests.' The priests
were ministers. God had said that when
lepers were made well they should go first
to the priests, to be looked at by them before they walked again about the streets.
So when these lepers heard Jesus tell them

to go to the priests, they knew that they should soon be quite well.

As they were walking along towards the place where the priests lived—they grew well. Those hands that were covered with white sores were now the same brown colour they had been before. When the lepers looked at each other they saw faces, that were of a sickly white, become rosy and healthy.

And when the lepers saw this, did they go on, or did they turn back?

One of them turned back, and only ONE; all the rest made haste to go to the priests.

Why did that one turn back?

It was that he might go to Jesus and thank Him. As he went along he praised God for His goodness with a loud voice. When he was sick he had asked to be cured with a loud voice, and now he was well he thanked God with a loud voice. This was right.

When he came to Jesus he fell down at His feet with his face to the ground, and thanked Him. Then Jesus said, 'Did not I cure ten lepers, but where are the nine? Only one has returned to praise God.'

Now Jesus knew that this man who had come back was not a Jew. He was a stranger, or a foreigner, and he came from a land where the people knew very little about God, yet he loved God better than the other lepers did. He was a Samaritan.

Is there a boy reading this book who was once in trouble? Did God get you out of trouble? Did you thank God? God knows your name. If you do not thank Him, He says, 'Where is that little boy, or that little girl? Why does not he come and thank Me? I have been very kind to him.'

Do you know the greatest kindness God has ever shown you? He has given His Son to die for your sins. Did you ever ONCE thank God for sending Jesus Christ to die upon the cross that you might not go to hell? If you have never thanked Him YET, begin this day, and say, 'O Father, I thank Thee for sending the Lord Jesus Christ to die upon the cross to save sinners.'

You may read this history in Luke, xvii, 11–19.

'How great is the love
    Which Jesus hath shown!
He came from above,
    From heaven's bright throne,
That He might deliver
    His children from hell,
And take them for ever
    In glory to dwell.

He died on the cross,
    And pour'd out His blood,
To bear their dread curse
    And fit them for God.
For love so amazing
    His name we adore,
And Him would be praising
    With saints evermore.'

Writer unknown

A CHILD'S THANKSGIVING.

'I prayed to God—He heard my prayer,
And made a little child His care;
When I was sick He heal'd my pain,
And gave me health and strength again.
Oh, let me now His grace implore,
And love and praise Him evermore.'

Writer unknown.

XXXV.

THE BLIND BEGGAR OF JERICHO.

Do not you pity the blind? How sad it must be never to see the light of the sun, nor the green leaves in spring, nor the faces of our dearest friends !

A long while ago a blind man sat begging by the side of the road. As he sat, he heard the noise of a great crowd walking along. He did not know why there was such a crowd, so he asked the people passing by why so many had come together. They told him that Jesus of Nazareth was passing that way.

The blind man had heard before of Jesus. He had heard that He could do great wonders, and he felt sure in his heart that Jesus could make him see. But the blind man could not go to Him—how could he dare to stir in such a crowd? he might have been pushed down and trodden upon, and crushed to death. But he could speak. He cried

out very loud, 'Have mercy on me, O Lord!'
He did not cry out once or twice, he kept
on crying out, hoping that Jesus would hear
him.

But the Lord took no notice of him, and
a great many people came up to him and
told him not to make such a noise. Yet
the poor man would not be quiet ; he knew
that the Lord was passing by, and that He
might soon be gone, and that He might
never pass by that way again—so he cried
out more than ever, 'Lord, have mercy on
me !'

And did the Lord take notice of him at
last ?

Yes, He did ; He stood still, and told the
people to bring that blind man to Him.
How kind it was in Jesus to care for the
blind beggar ! Jesus is very kind, and cares
for every poor creature in the world.

At last the blind man heard some one
say, 'Be of good comfort ; rise, He calleth
thee.'

He got up very quickly, and went to Jesus
for now the people made room for him.

R

No one now was rude to the poor beggar, for Jesus had called for him.

And what did Jesus say to him?

He asked him this question, 'What do you wish Me to do for you?'

The man replied, 'Lord, that I may received my sight.'

Jesus pitied him very much, and He touched his eyes, and said, 'Receive thy sight.'

That moment he was able to see.

How glad he now was that he had cried out, 'Lord, have mercy on me,' and that he had not left off when the people told him not to make a noise! He would not leave Jesus now he had found Him, but went after Him on the road, praising Him, and thanking God for His goodness.

If all people would pray as this blind man did, Jesus would hear them all. The child who reads this book is not blind. If you were blind, how could you read to your father or mother? But there is something which Jesus could do for you, that would make you happy for ever. What is it? Do you know? If He were to say, 'What do you wish Me to do for you?'—what would you answer? Would you say, 'Forgive me my sins, and give me Thy Holy Spirit?' My dear child, do make this little prayer every day. Jesus would hear you. He would be much pleased to hear you praying to Him, because He loves you, and He once died upon the cross that you might not go to hell. If you go to heaven you will see the blind beggar there—I mean, the beggar who once was blind. Then you will sing with him about the love of Jesus in saving your souls.

Read Mark, x, 46 to end; and also Luke, xviii, 35 to end.

'The blind man in his darkness,
  Beside the highway sat;
He heard the trampling footstep
  Throng to the city gate.
They told him, Christ of Nazareth
  That hour was passing by;
And, "Jesus, have Thou mercy!"
  Was then the blind man's cry.'

                              NEALE.

XXXVL.

THE MAN IN THE TREE.

SOMETIMES the Queen passes through the city of London in her grand carriage of state. Then all the windows in the streets, from the shop to the garret, are full of faces looking out and longing to have a peep at Her Majesty the Queen.

More than eighteen hundred years ago, the King of kings was walking about this world. It is true, He did not go in a grand carriage drawn by fine horses, — no, He was a poor man, and He walked about from place to place: but then He spoke such sweet words that people came from far to hear Him; and, besides this, He did such wonders — making the blind to see and the lame to walk — that every one wished to look at Him.

There was a man who longed and tried to see this great King, but he could not; because there was a crowd all round, and he

was a short man, and he could not look
over the heads of the people. So he ran on
a little way, and then he climbed up into a
tree called a sycamore tree, which is a high
tree with strong branches and large leaves.

There he waited till the King passed by.
He thought he should see Him well from
this high place.

How much surprised he was when Jesus
came to the place! (for this King was the
Lord Jesus.) The Lord looked up towards
the tree. Now, the man could see Him well
—not only the hair upon His head, but His
eyes, and His whole face.

Jesus not only looked up, but stopped and
spoke. He said, 'Zaccheus, make haste
and come down, for to-day I must stay at
thy house.' Jesus knew the man's name;
He knew why he had gone up into the tree,
and He knew that he had a house in the
next town.

Zaccheus did not stop any longer in the
tree; he got down very fast, went back to
his house, and was ready to receive the Lord
into it. He thought it a great honour to

receive such a visitor beneath his roof, and, indeed, it was the greatest honour he could have; even an angel would think it a great honour to have a visit from the Son of God.

Why did He choose to come to the house of Zaccheus? Because He had determined to make Zaccheus happy for ever. Once Zaccheus had been a wicked man; he had cheated many people. It was his business to collect the *public* taxes, and for this reason he was called a *publican*: but he had not been honest; he had charged more than he ought, and he had grown rich by his dishonesty. His cheating ways had been found out, and now he had a bad character; so, when people saw Jesus go into his house, many said, 'Why does He go into the house of a wicked person?'

But the people who said *that* did not know that Jesus came into the world to save sinners. Zaccheus was now very sorry for his past wickedness, and while Jesus was in his house, he stood and said to the Lord, 'Behold, Lord, I give half of my goods to the poor, and I will give back to those people from whom I have taken too much *four* times what I have taken.'

Was not this right of Zaccheus?

Everybody whom he had cheated might come to him and say, 'You took from me one penny, or twopence, more than you ought, will you give me back four times as much?' If the people said true, then Zaccheus would give them back the money.

Jesus was much pleased to hear Zaccheus speak as he did. He praised him, and said, he was a son of Abraham. Abraham was a man who believed in God, and Jesus saw that Zaccheus did so also, for He could see into his heart. These were the words that Jesus spoke to Zaccheus: 'This day is salvation come to this house, forsomuch as he also is a son of Abraham.'

I do not know whether Zaccheus had any little children,—but if he had, how glad they must have been to hear Jesus say salvation was come to the house (or the family)! How happy are the children of a man who believes in Jesus! A good father prays for his children, teaches them, takes them to the house of God, and begs them to be good and to love Christ.

Zaccheus never could forget the visit that Jesus had made to his family. How often he would talk of it, and call to mind all that Jesus had done and said! How often he would repeat the sweet sentence, 'The Son of man is come to seek and to save that which was lost!'

Jesus is not now walking about the world, but many of His servants are, and they go like Him to seek the lost. They go to the houses of sinners; they go to the rooms of sinners; they stand by the dying beds of sinners, and tell them of the Saviour.

You may find the history of Zaccheus in Luke, xix, 1–10.

A CHILD'S PRAYER.

Oh, sweet Shepherd, gently lead me,
Lest I fall, or go astray:
With the bread of Heaven feed me,
That I faint not by the way.'

Writer unknown

XXXVII.

CHRIST IN THE GARDEN.

WHEN the Lord Jesus lived in this world He used often to go into a garden full of large trees.

When He sat in the garden His disciples would sit with Him and listen to His sweet words about His Father in heaven.

I will now tell you about the last time that the Lord Jesus went to the garden before He died.

It was in the evening, when it was dark. All His friends were with Him except one, and that one was Judas: he was gone away from Jesus. But there were eleven men still with their Lord, and they loved Him very much. They knew that He was very unhappy that evening, and they were unhappy too.

What made Jesus sad? It was this: men had sinned, and done very wickedly, and they deserved to be punished, for God must punish sin; but Jesus had come into the world to die for their sins. Oh, was not this kind of Jesus Christ, to die for sinners such as you and I? And was it not kind of God His Father to give up His only Son to suffer pain and grief, that we might not suffer pain and grief for ever and ever?

Now you see why Jesus was sad. He was going to die for our sins; the time was almost come; this was His last evening. He had come into the garden to pray to His Father.

When the Lord was at the garden-gate He said to His friends, ' Sit here, while I go and pray a little way off.' He took three of His friends with Him, but He left eight near the garden-gate.

Should you like to know the names of the three who went with Jesus? They were Peter, and James, and John. They often were with Jesus when no one else was there besides.

When the Lord had gone some way, He said to Peter, James, and John, ' My soul is exceeding sorrowful, even unto death; stay

here and watch.' Then He went a very little way off, and lay with His face on the ground, and began to pray to His Father; and these were the words He said: 'O My Father, if it be possible, let this cup pass from Me.'

What did He mean by this cup? He did not mean a real cup. It was not a cup of bitter medicine He was going to drink, but a cup of pain and grief, and He asked His Father not to let Him drink it. But then He knew that His Father loved us sinners, and wished to save us; so Jesus finished His prayer in these words: 'Not as I will, but as Thou wilt.'

What a sweet prayer this was! Jesus did not wish to do His own will, but His Father's will. When we pray to God in our troubles, let us say the same: 'Not as I will, but as Thou wilt.'

After Jesus had prayed He went to His three friends, but He found them sleeping, for they were very much tired, and very unhappy. He was not angry, but He said to them gently, 'Could ye not watch with

Me one hour?' Then He went back again to pray, and He said the same words He had said before.

After He had prayed He returned to His friends, but He found them asleep, and when He spoke to them they did not know what to answer Him. They knew they ought to have been praying and watching with their Lord.

Jesus went back again to pray the third time.

His Father heard His prayers, and He sent an angel from heaven to comfort Him.

What a sad sight the angel saw when he came down and found Jesus in the garden! The Son of God was in such great sorrow, that the blood came through his skin while He prayed, and it fell on the ground in great drops. Oh, what pain the blessed Saviour must have felt! It was for *us*, and not for the angel, He was suffering all this pain. That angel had never sinned, but we have sinned every day and every hour.

After Jesus had prayed very earnestly, He came back the third time to His friends

Were they sleeping still? Yes, they **were**; **they** had not seen the bright angel talking to their Lord. This time Jesus said to His three friends, 'Rise up, and let us go.' He told them that the people **who** hated **Him** were coming.

While Jesus was yet speaking, a number of men came near, with lamps in their hands, and great sticks, and swords.

And who was showing them the way? It was the wicked Judas. He had often been in the garden with his Master, and he knew where to find Him. The Lord let the wicked people take hold of Him.

Oh, what a loving Saviour Jesus was! **Now** He is alive again, and is ready to hear our prayers, and to pardon our sins, and to give us new hearts, and to take us to heaven.

This history **may** be found in Matt. xxvi, 36-47; Mark, xiv, 32-43; Luke, xxii, 39-47; John, xviii, 1-4.

THE LOST SHEEP.

THERE were ninety-and-nine that safely lay
  In the shelter of the fold ;
And one was out on the hills away,
  Far off from the gates of gold ;
Away on the mountains wild and bare,
Away from the tender Shepherd's care.

Lord, Thou hast here the ninety-and-nine,
  Are these not enough for Thee ?
But the Shepherd made answer 'This of Mine
  Has wandered away from Me :
And, although the roads be rough and steep,
I go to the desert to find My sheep.'

But none of the ransomed ever knew
  How deep were the waters crossed ;
Nor how dark the night that the Lord passed through
  Ere He found the sheep that was lost.
Out in the desert He heard its cry,
Sick, and helpless, and ready to die.

Lord, whence are those blood-drops all the way
  That mark out the mountain track ?'
'They were shed for one who had gone astray
  Ere the Shepherd could bring him back.'
'Lord, whence are Thy hands so rent and torn ?'
'They were pierced to-night by many a thorn.'

And all through the mountains, thunder riven
  And up from the rocky steep,
There arose a cry to the gates of heaven,
  'Rejoice, I have found My sheep !'
And the angels echoed around the throne,
'Rejoice, for the Lord brings back His own !'

Little Sower.

XXXVIII.

THE MAN WHO SAT BY THE FIRE IN THE HALL.

SOMETIMES Jesus used to say to His twelve disciples, 'I shall soon die; wicked men will kill Me; they will nail Me on a cross; but I shall rise again out of My grave.' The disciples were very sorry to hear their Master talk in this way; they could not bear to think that He should die.

Once Peter said, 'I will go to prison with you. I will die with you.' Then Jesus said to Peter, 'Will you do so? No, this night you will say three times over that you do not know Me; you will say so three times before the cock has crowed twice.'

Jesus was God, and knew all that was going to happen. Peter could not believe that he would ever say he did not know his dear Master, but Peter did not know how much naughtiness there was in his heart.

That very night some wicked men came
into a garden where Jesus was, and bound
Him with ropes, and took Him to a great
house. The judges were seated on high seats
in that great house or hall.

Peter was very sorry to see his Master
taken away, and he went after Him. He
did not go with Him, but he followed Him
some way off. There was a woman at the
door, and she let him go in; then Peter
sat by a fire, and warmed himself.

Soon the woman who had let Peter in
looked at him, and said, 'Are you not one of
the disciples of Jesus?' Then Peter was
afraid lest the wicked people should use him
ill, as they did his Master, and he said to
the woman, 'Woman, I know Him not!'
That was a lie—a dreadful lie!

Presently afterwards Peter left the hall,
and went out in the porch. Then the cock
crew. Did Peter remember what Jesus had
said? No, he did not; he took no notice of
the crowing of the cock.

While he was in the porch a man said to
him, 'You are one of the disciples of

Jesus.' Peter answered, 'Man, I am not!' and not content with saying this, he soon began to swear he did not know the Lord.

He returned into the great house. There his Master was. The wicked people were round Him, laughing at Him, beating Him, and even spitting at Him. Several persons came up to Peter, and said, 'You are one of this man's disciples.' Then he began to curse and swear, and to say, 'I do not know the man!' While he was speaking in this wicked manner, the cock crew again, and Jesus Himself turned towards Peter, and looked at him. Now Peter remembered what Jesus had said to him; now he felt very sorry, indeed, for his wickedness. He left the hall, and began to weep very bitterly. He thought over all that had happened—how kind his Master had been to him, and how ungratefully he had behaved. Could he ever forget that look which Jesus had cast upon him? What sort of look do you think it was—an angry look, or a sorrowful look?

I think there was more sorrow than anger in it.

Did the Lord Jesus forgive Peter his great sin? Yes, He did. The next day Jesus was crucified and was buried. But He lay only three days in His grave. One morning, very early, He rose again. How glad Peter was to see Him again! Jesus did *not* say to Peter, 'I cannot love you any more, because you behaved so ill that night.' No, Jesus said to him, 'Do you love Me?' And Peter said, 'Yes, Lord, you know I do.' Jesus asked him three times if he loved Him, and Peter said three times over that he did love Him.

Jesus is now in heaven with God His Father, and Peter is there too.

Jesus wants you to love Him. He has been very kind to you; He made your body, for He is God. He died on the cross to save you from going to hell. Do you love Him? How wicked it would be not to love Him! It is very wicked not to love your father or your mother, but it is more wicked still not to love Jesus.

When you do wrong Jesus sees you, and if you are sorry for your sin, and cry about it, Jesus sees your tears. Children who really love Jesus are very sorry when they have done wrong. Did you ever cry because you had displeased God? You have often cried—what has it been about? Was it because you were cold and hungry? Was it because you had pain in your head? Was it because a boy had taken away your things? Was it because your father was angry with you? Was it because you were disappointed of a treat? I dare say you have cried for all these reasons.

Have you ever cried about your sins? It is a good day when a boy or a girl sits in some corner, and thinks over sins that are past, and feels sorry, and prays to God, and says, 'O God, forgive me for the sake of Jesus who died upon the cross, and give me Thy Holy Spirit to make me good.'

You may read the history of Peter's sin in Matt. xxvi, 69 to end; Mark, xiv, 66 to end; Luke, xxii, 54–62; John, xviii, 15–27.

XXXIX.

THE MAN WHO HANGED HIMSELF.

I AM going to tell you the history of a very wicked man named Judas. He was a liar, a thief, and a murderer; and, worse than all, he was a hypocrite; that is, he was a man who pretended to be good. But though Judas was so wicked, the Son of God chose him to be one of the twelve men who lived with Him. Are you not surprised to hear this? Jesus knew that Judas was wicked, yet He let him come after Him. Jesus often talked to him, and told him about His Father in heaven. Jesus was very kind to him, yet Judas did not love Jesus.

The other disciples thought that Judas was good; they all put their money into one bag, and they let Judas take care of that bag; they did not know that he often took the money out of it, and kept it himself. Judas was a thief, but he was not found out for a long time. Jesus knew that he was a thief, because He knows all things.

Once a good woman named **Mary** poured some very sweet stuff upon the head of Jesus, and upon His **feet**. This ointment was in a beautiful white **box**, but Mary broke the box to pour it out upon Jesus. When Judas saw what she had done, he said it was a great pity she had wasted the ointment upon Jesus, and that it would have been better to sell it and give the money to the poor.

But had Mary wasted the ointment? Oh, no; it was not too good to be given to the Son of God : nothing could be too good for Him, who is all goodness.

But why did Judas wish the ointment had been sold? **His** reason was, that he thought the money would have been put into the bag for him to give to the poor, and then he could have stolen some of it. He pretended to care for the poor, for he was very sly. Jesus knew all that Judas was thinking about, and He said that Mary had done right in pouring the ointment upon His head.

Then Judas was very angry because Jesus had taken Mary's part, and he went out of the room. And where did he go? To some wicked men, who wanted to kill Jesus. It was night, and these wicked men were saying to each other, 'How shall we get hold of Jesus, that we may have Him killed? In the day we are afraid of taking Him, because the people like Him very much, and we do not know where He goes at night.' Judas came in and said to the wicked men, 'I will show you where Jesus goes at night.' Then the wicked men were pleased, and promised to give Judas thirty pieces of silver.

Two days afterwards Jesus took His last supper with His twelve disciples. Judas was there. Jesus told His disciples that He should soon die. All the disciples, except Judas, were very sorry to hear Him say this. Then Jesus said, 'One of you will betray Me.' What did He mean? He meant that one of His disciples would show the wicked people where He went at night. Then each of the disciples said, 'Is it I?' And at last Judas said, 'Is it I?' Then Jesus said that it was.

Soon afterwards Jesus said to Judas, 'Do quickly what you are going to do.' Then Judas got up, and went out of the room. The other disciples thought he was gone to buy something at the shop, or to give something to the poor, but he was gone to the wicked people. He knew where Jesus was going that night, and he meant to bring the wicked people there.

After Judas was gone, Jesus left the room and went down-stairs, and walked along the streets. His disciples went with Him. They came at last to a garden full of high trees. There they used often to go with Jesus.

This night Jesus went alone to one part of the garden, and prayed to His Father. He was very unhappy. At last He came back to His disciples.

Just at that moment a number of men were seen with lamps in their hands

Judas showed them the way: he went up to Jesus and kissed Him. Why did he kiss Him? Only to show the men which was Jesus. How very wicked it was to pretend to love Jesus while he helped people to kill Him! Jesus knew why he kissed Him, but He spoke very gently to him and said, 'Friend, why are you come?' The wicked people seized Jesus, bound Him with ropes, and said He must come with them. Then all the disciples were frightened, and ran away.

The wicked men made Jesus stand before them all the night. In the morning they said that He must be killed.

He was nailed to a cross of wood till He died. Oh what a painful death this was! But Jesus came down from heaven that He might die instead of us. If He had not died, we should all have gone to hell; but now, if we love Jesus, we shall go to heaven. How kind it was of Jesus to die for sinners such as you and me! Ought we not to love Him?

When Judas heard that the wicked men

had said that Jesus must be killed, he was very sorry. He did not like to keep the thirty pieces of silver. He felt he had behaved very wickedly to his kind, good Master, the Lord Jesus. What could he do with the money? He did not like to keep it: he did not like to spend it; so he took it back to the men who gave it to him. He said, 'I have done very wrong; Jesus is good, and I have betrayed Him to be killed.' But the wicked men were not sorry—they did not care—so Judas threw down the pieces of silver, and went away.

Where did he go? If he had gone and prayed, God would have forgiven him, for He pardons all who are really sorry for their sins. But Judas did not pray. He felt very unhappy, so he thought he would kill himself. It is very wicked for a man to kill himself. Judas went into a field and hanged himself. Everybody who lived in the town heard of it, and they called the place where Judas died 'The Field of Blood.'

And what became of the soul of Judas? He went to his father the devil, to be tormented in hell for ever and ever. It would have been good for Judas if he had never been born. Had his parents known when he was a little baby what a wicked man he would grow up, oh, how sorry they would have been!

I hope your parents will never be sorry that you were born. I hope that you your self will never be sorry that you were born The wicked in hell wish that they had never been born. It is a good thing to be born if we go to heaven when we die. Pray to God to forgive you all your sins, and to make you like an angel.

You will find part of Judas's history in Matt. xxvi, 47–50; xxvii, 1–10.

XL.

THE JUDGE.

HAVE you ever seen a judge upon his high seat, judging a thief or a murderer? Many people crowd into the place when a bad man is taken before the judge.

Once a very good man was taken before a judge; there were some wicked people who hated this good man, and who wanted to have Him killed; so they brought Him to the judge early one morning.

Do you know who this good man was? He was the Son of God, come from heaven to live in this world for a little while.

Who was the judge? His name was Pontius Pilate; he knew nothing about God; he was a heathen, and had been taught to worship idols. Pilate thought that Jesus was good, and he said to the wicked men who brought Him, 'I find no fault in Him.'

Then the wicked men were more angry,

and said that Jesus had done a great many wrong things. While they were speaking, Jesus said nothing; He was as meek as a lamb, and they were as fierce as lions and tigers.

It was the rich people who hated Jesus the most. Pilate thought that perhaps the poor people would wish Him to be set free. It was the custom to let one prisoner loose every year. Pilate said to the people, 'Which shall I release, Jesus or Barabbas?' Now this Barabbas was a robber and a murderer. The people answered, 'Barabbas.' It was the rich and great men who had persuaded the people to ask for Barabbas. How shocking it was to hear crowds of people crying out with loud voices in the street, 'Not this man, but Barabbas!' Jesus had been very kind to the people; He had cured the sick, and blind, and lame; and He had taught the poor all day long about God: and yet now they cried out, 'Away with this man, and release unto us Barabbas!'

Pilate was sorry to hear them speak in

this way, and he said, 'What shall I do to Jesus?' They cried out, 'Crucify Him! crucify Him!' They wanted Him to be nailed on a cross of wood till He died. Oh, how cruel!

While Pilate was on his judgment-seat his wife sent a message to him. It was to tell him not to hurt Jesus, for that He was good, and that she had been dreaming a very sad dream about Him. That was a good message. God had sent the dreams to Pilate's wife. Do you not hope that Pilate will mind his wife's advice? He wished to mind it, but when the people went on crying out, 'Crucify Him! crucify Him!' he was afraid to say, 'No,' lest they should be angry with him. But if Pilate had done right, God would have taken care of him, and made him happy for ever.

At last Pilate took some water and washed his hands while everybody was looking at him. Why? Not to make his hands clean, but to show the wicked men that he was clean from the blood of Jesus.

But could water wash his *heart* clean from wickedness?

Then Pilate gave Jesus up to be crucified, and he let Barabbas go out of prison. How wicked it was of Pilate to do so! He knew better: he knew he was doing wrong.

Before Jesus was crucified He was scourged; that is, His back was beaten with hard ropes full of knots. Yet Jesus bore all the pain as meekly as a lamb.

After He had been scourged, He was tormented by the soldiers. Hundreds of cruel soldiers came round Him and took off His clothes, and put on Him some fine clothes, like those which kings wear, only just to laugh at Him; and they took some thorns, and made a crown and put it on His head. You know that thorns are very sharp, and prick very much. How could the cruel men put thorns on that dear head! Then they took a reed and put it in His hand for a sceptre, such as kings hold, and then knelt down to Him, and said, 'Hail, King of the Jews!' How dreadful it must have been to hear the laughter of those soldiers! But they did more than laugh; they were so wicked as to beat Him on His head. and to spit in His face.

Pilate saw Jesus, and He showed Him to the people once more. Jesus came out of the great house where the soldiers had been tormenting Him, dressed in His purple clothes, with His crown of thorns on His head. Pilate said to the people, 'Behold your King!' But did the sight melt their hard hearts? Oh, no; they still cried out, 'Crucify Him! crucify Him!' Then Pilate gave Him up to be crucified.

You may read part of the history of Pontius Pilate in Matt. xxvii, 11–31: John, xix, 1–7.

'Little children, praise the Saviour;
He regards you from above:
Praise Him for His great salvation,
Praise Him for His precious love!
Sweet hosannas
To the name of Jesus sing.

There is a green hill far away,
  Without a city wall,
Where the dear Lord was crucified.
  Who died to save us all.

We may not know, we cannot tell,
  What pains He had to bear;
But we believe it was for us,
  He hung and suffered there.

He died that we might be forgiven,
  He died to make us good,
That we might go at last to heaven,
  Saved by His precious blood.

There was no other good enough,
  To pay the price of sin,
He only could unlock the gate
  Of heaven, and let us in.

O dearly, dearly has He loved,
  And we must love Him too,
And trust in His redeeming blood,
  And try His works to do.

XLI.

CHRIST ON THE CROSS.

WHEN a great prince dies, and his body is carried to the tomb, how many wish to see the funeral! There is the hearse, covered with nodding plumes, and there is the train of coaches, all drawn by black horses; but the coffin is hidden, and the dead man's body is not seen. Oh, could we see it, so stiff and so pale, we should be shocked at the sight!

I am going to tell you of a much sadder sight than this.

There was a crowd of people looking at one man; that man was covered with blood; His back was marked by the stripes of the rope; His forehead was pricked by thorns which had been fastened round His head; His face looked very sad, as if He had been shedding many tears; His body was very thin, and His knees were so weak that He could hardly stand; yet there was a great piece of wood on His back, and He was dragging it along, but it seemed as if He would faint and drop down dead by the way.

There were some soldiers near the man —very cruel men, who laughed at Him and abused Him. But they did not wish Him to die on the road, for they were going to kill Him in another place; they would not help Him to drag the wood along, but they met a stranger, and they desired him to help to carry the wood.

All the crowd were not laughing at the poor man; some were crying very much. There were some women, who seemed very unhappy; these women loved the poor man, and could not bear to see Him ill-treated.

Do you think that poor man is good? See how gentle He looks! Now hear Him speak! How sweetly He speaks! He turns round and tells the poor women not to cry about Him.

Not one rough word does that poor man say to all the wicked people who are laugh-

I . N . R . I .

ing at Him. Do you not think He must be good?

At last the soldiers come to a place outside the town; they lay the wood on the ground; it is a very great piece of wood, and there is another piece nailed across it. It is a cross.

The soldiers take off the poor man's clothes, and then they make Him lie upon the cross; they stretch out His hands, and strike a great nail through each palm; they stretch out His legs, and strike great nails through His feet, and so they fasten Him to the wood: then they take hold of the cross and lift it up, and thrust it into the ground. Oh, what a jerk that was for those bleeding wounds in those hands and feet!

It is morning, about nine o'clock; it is beginning to get hot, for the weather is hot.

What a crowd collects round that cross! What loud laughs are heard! Some people say, 'Why does He not come down from the cross? for He said He was the Son of God.'

And is He the Son of God?

Oh, yes, He is; He came down from heaven to die instead of you and me, my child. We all deserve to die, for we are wicked. But the Son of God never did anything wrong.

What is He saying upon the cross? This is what He says: 'Father, forgive them, for they know not what they do.' How kind to pray for the people who were killing Him!

The soldiers do not pity Him. What are they doing with those clothes? They are dividing them between them; the four soldiers tear the clothes into four parts: there is one garment, something like a shirt, only with no seam in it, but woven all in one piece; the soldiers do not like to tear *that*, so they cast lots for it, to see who will get it. These soldiers care for the clothes, but not for the Son of God.

Oh, foolish soldiers! that poor man whom you laugh at could give you better clothes than those—clothes that would never wear out. All the people who love the Son of

God shall live with Him, and wear white and beautiful clothes.

At last it is twelve o'clock in the day; all at once it grows quite dark, though it is the middle of the day. No one now can see the face of Jesus. Do you not think the darkness must frighten the wicked people? It is a sign that God is angry.

Still the people go on mocking—they are not sorry for their cruelty.

At last a voice is heard to say, 'I thirst!'

It is the voice of Jesus. He must be thirsty, hanging for six hours upon that cross in the heat, and in great pain.

One of the soldiers dips a sponge in vinegar and puts it on the end of a branch, and lifts it up to the mouth of Jesus—it touches His dry lips—then a voice is heard again, saying, 'It is finished!' that means, it is all done.

Once more a loud voice is heard. It is Jesus praying to His Father to take His soul, and then He bows His head and dies.

Then the earth shakes, and great cracks

are seen in the hard rocks, and the wicked people are very much afraid.

Then it becomes light, and every one can see the dead body of Jesus hanging on the cross.

His pain is over; His sorrow is gone; He is happy now, and He will be happy for ever. His body is put into the ground, but it soon rises out of the tomb, and goes up to God the Father.

There are a great many souls with Jesus in heaven now. All who love Him go up to be with Him when they die, but the wicked are cast down into darkness with the devil. May you never go there! Jesus died to save you, but if you will go on being wicked He cannot save you. How glad Jesus is when any boy or girl says to Him, 'Jesus, save me!'

Would you read about the death of Jesus? Look at Matt. xxvii, 31–54; Mark, xv, 20–39; Luke, xxiii, 26–48; John, xix, 16–30.

'I lay my sins on Jesus,
　The spotless Lamb of God;
He bears them all and frees us
　From the accursed load.
I bring my guilt to Jesus,
　To wash my crimson stains
White in His blood most precious,
　Till not a spot remains.

I lay my wants on Jesus,
　All fulness dwells in Him;
He heals all my diseases,
　He doth my soul redeem.
I lay my griefs on Jesus,
　My burdens and my cares;
He from them all releases,
　He all my sorrows shares.

I rest my soul on Jesus —
　This weary soul of mine;
His right hand me embraces,
　I on His breast recline.
I love the name of Jesus —
　Immanuel — Christ — the Lord!
Like fragrance on the breezes
　His name is spread abroad.

I long to be like Jesus —
　Meek, loving, lowly, mild;
I long to be like Jesus —
　The Father's holy child.

I long to be with Jesus,
  Amid the heavenly throng,
To sing with saints His praises,
  To learn the angels' song.'

BONAR.

A LITTLE CHILD'S PRAYER.

'Jesus, tender Saviour,
  Hast Thou died for me •
Make me very thankful
  In my heart to Thee.

When the sad, sad story
  Of Thy grief I read,
Make me very sorry
  For my sin indeed.

Now I know Thou livest,
  And dost plead for me,
Make me very thankful
  In my prayers to Thee.

Soon I hope in glory
  At Thy side to stand;
Make me fit to meet Thee
  In that happy land.'

F. P.

XLII.

THE DYING THIEF.

SOME people fall sick, lie upon their beds, and die there. Some people meet with an accident, and are suddenly killed—they are burned, they are drowned, they are crushed under a wheel, or kicked by a horse, or dashed to pieces by a fall. Some people are put to death; they are accused of having murdered one of their fellow-creatures, and are hanged up by the neck till they die. Which of all these ways of dying is most dreadful? Is it not the last? It is dreadful to be put to death on account of crimes we have done.

Sometimes good people are put to death. Wicked people accuse them, and the judge believes the accusers, and orders them to be executed.

The Son of God once became a man. Wicked men hated Him, accused Him, and killed Him!

The body of Jesus hung upon the cross, and the nails tore the tender flesh of His hands and feet. Thus the Lord was crucified.

There were two other men nailed upon crosses in the same place as Jesus. They were wicked men ; they were thieves. They were crucified on each side of Jesus—one on the right hand, and the other on the left; they were very near Him, and they could speak to Him, and hear what He said. They saw the men passing by the cross of Jesus, and looking up and laughing; they heard them reading what was written over the cross, 'This is the King of the Jews;' and they heard them say, 'If He be the Son of God, let Him come down from the cross;' and they heard Jesus sweetly say, 'Father, forgive them, for they know not what they do!'

And what did the thieves do when they saw and heard these things? One of the thieves began to mock and abuse Jesus, and he said, 'If Thou be the Christ, save Thyself and us.' That was not a good prayer. The thief asked Jesus to save him.

but he did not believe He could save him; he wanted to be saved from dying on the cross, but he did not care about being saved from the everlasting pains of hell.

The other thief was quite different. He was displeased to hear his fellow talk in this wicked way just as he was dying, and he spoke to him; for, though the cross of Jesus was between them, he could speak loud enough to make the other thief hear.

He said, 'Do you not fear God now that you are condemned to die? We deserve to die, but this man hath done nothing wrong.'

You see that this thief was sorry for his sins; you see, also, that he believed that Jesus was quite good. I do not know what the other thief said to him, or whether he gave him any answer.

The thief who was sorry for his sins then spoke to Jesus. This was his prayer: 'Lord, remember me when Thou comest into Thy kingdom.' The dying thief believed that Jesus was a King, and that He would one day sit upon a throne.

Did Jesus grant the poor thief's prayer?

He gave him such an answer as will surprise you, if you have never heard it before. He said, 'To-day shalt thou be with Me in Paradise!'

What is Paradise? It is a happy place. That very day the poor thief was to be there with Jesus.

What a happy thing it was for that poor thief that his cross was placed so near the cross of Jesus! Had not the thief been nailed to that cross, he might never have seen Jesus, he might never have believed in Him, he might never have prayed to Him, he might never have gone to live with Him.

Was it long before that poor thief died? Not long: but Jesus died first. His last words were, 'It is finished!' and then He died at three o'clock in the afternoon. It was at nine in the morning that He had been nailed to the cross.

The thieves were still hanging alive on their crosses, when some soldiers came to see whether they were dead. When the soldiers saw that the thieves were alive, they broke their legs, and the pain killed them immediately.

Then the thief who loved Jesus went to be with Him. How glad the angels were to see the sinner saved for ever! It was Jesus who had saved him. If Jesus had not died upon the cross, that thief must have been lost.* It was the blood of Jesus that washed him from his sins; it was the Spirit of Jesus that made his heart sorry, and taught his tongue to pray.

But was it for that thief only that Jesus died? Oh, no; He died for all the thieves who ever have believed in Him, and who ever shall believe in Him. It is a wretched thing to be a thief; God has said, 'Thou shalt not steal,' and all who go on stealing will be lost. But if, when thieves hear of Jesus, they are sorry for their wickedness, and ask Him to forgive them, they shall be saved.

If any sinner, when he hears this history, thinks in his heart, 'I will go on stealing till I am *just* going to die, and then I will be sorry and ask God to pardon me,' *that*

* Rev. xxi, 8.

sinner is in great danger of being sent to hell. God is very angry with him for intending to go on in his wickedness. I do not know what God will do to him, but He has cut off many sinners quite suddenly: He has taken them away in His anger, and given them at last no time to repent.

The history of the dying thief is to be found in Luke, xxiii, 32, 33, 39–43; John, xix, 30–37.

'Lo! at noon 'tis sudden night,
   Darkness covers all the sky!
Rocks are rending at the sight!
   Children, can you tell me why?
What can all these wonders be?
Jesus dies at Calvary!

Nailed upon the cross, behold
   How His tender limbs are torn!
For a royal crown of gold,
   They have made Him one of thorn
Cruel hands, that dare to bind
Thorns upon a brow so kind!

See! the blood is falling fast
   From His forehead and His side.
Hark! He now has breathed His last,
   With a mighty groan He died!
Children, shall I tell you why
Jesus condescends to die?

He, who was a King above
   Left His kingdom for a grave,
Out of pity and of love,
   That the guilty He might save·
Down to this sad world He flew
For such little ones as you!

You were wretched, weak, and vile,
   You deserv'd His holy frown;
But He saw you with a smile,
   And to save you hasten'd down.
Listen, children! this is why
Jesus condescends to die.

Come then, children, come and see,
   Lift your little hands to pray:
" Blessed Jesus, pardon me,
   Help a guilty infant," say;
" Since it was for such as I
Thou didst condescend to die." '

JANE TAYLOR.

XLIII.

CHRIST IN THE TOMB.

You have heard that the Lord Jesus Christ was nailed upon the cross till He died.

Do you know what was done with His dead body?

There was a rich man who loved Jesus; his name was Joseph; he went to the judge, and said, 'Do let me have the body of Jesus who has been crucified.' And the judge said, 'Yes, you may have it.'

It was right of Joseph not to be ashamed to ask for the body. It was thought a great disgrace to be crucified. Now, you know, it is a disgrace to be hanged, because it is murderers who are hanged. But, though Jesus had never done one sin, He was crucified, as if He had been a bad man. Joseph knew He was good; though people spoke against Him, Joseph loved Him still.

Joseph was very glad when he got leave to have the body of his Lord.

Another rich man went with Joseph; he was called Nicodemus.

Joseph and Nicodemus went together to the cross, and took the nails out of the hands of Jesus, and the nails out of His feet. What marks were left in those dear hands and feet! How the blood had run down from the wound in His side! It is *that* blood which can wash our souls clean from all sin. Jesus shed it that sinners might be forgiven, and made good and holy.

In what was the body put when it was taken down from the cross? Not in a coffin; Joseph and his friends wrapped it in a clean, fine, white linen sheet; and they wrapped up with it a quantity of very nice sweet-smelling spices: it was a mixture of myrrh and aloes. But first they bound a cloth round His head—that head which the thorns had pierced.

Then they carried the bleeding body into a garden very near the cross. In this garden there was a rock, which was hard like stone. In the side of the rock there was a great hole—or cave. Joseph had once ordered this cave to be made. And why? That he might be buried there himself when he died. But now he was going to lay the body of Jesus in this cave.

It was a sweet tomb, for no dead body had ever been laid there before. Joseph was glad that the Son of God should lie in his own grave. There was no door to it, so Joseph had a very great stone rolled before the mouth of the cave, that no beast or bird might come in to devour the precious body, and that no wicked man might steal it, and carry it away.

It was just as the sun was setting that the body of our beloved Saviour was laid in the tomb.

That night His friends shed many bitter tears, for they thought they should never see Him again in this world.

But Jesus could not remain in the grave; His body could not corrupt, or turn to dust. And why not? Because He had done no sin. Our bodies turn to dust when we die, because we are sinners. But Jesus had borne the punishment of our sins, and now all was over, and His spirit was with His Father in heaven, and His wounded body was resting for a little while in a sweet tomb, soon to rise again.

It is a blessed thing for us that Jesus lay in *that* tomb. We need not be afraid to be put in the ground, as Jesus Himself was buried. Is the grave dark? The love of Jesus makes it light. Is the grave cold? The love of Jesus makes it warm. Is the grave loathsome? The love of Jesus makes it sweet. Is the grave hard? The love of Jesus makes it soft. The grave is a bed for the bodies of God's children. They shall not always lie there. As Jesus rose, so shall they rise, and when they rise they shall be like Him — beautiful, glorious, holy, and happy.

On the third day the Son of God rose from the dead, and now He sits at the right hand of His Father, and He will come again to raise the dead, and to judge the world.

'All that are in the graves shall hear His voice, and shall come forth: they that have done good, unto the resurrection of life; and they that have done evil, unto the resurrection of damnation.' (John, v, 29.)

You will find accounts of the burial of the Lord Jesus Christ in Matt. xxvii, 57–61; Mark, xv, 42–46; Luke, xxiii, 50–53; John, xix, 38 to end.

HYMN FOR TWO CHILDREN.

(Each to say one line by turns.)

FIRST CHILD.

'Who came from heaven to ransom us?

SECOND CHILD.

Jesus, who died upon the tree.

FIRST CHILD.

Why did He come from heaven above?

SECOND CHILD.

He came because His name was "Love."

FIRST CHILD.

And did He die—the Son of God?

SECOND CHILD.

Yes, on the cross He shed His blood.

FIRST CHILD.

Why did my Lord and Saviour bleed?

SECOND CHILD.

That we from evil might be freed.

FIRST CHILD.

When He had died, what happened then?

SECOND CHILD.

On the third day He rose again.

FIRST CHILD.

Where did He go when He had risen?

SECOND CHILD.

He went to God's right hand in heaven.

FIRST CHILD.

Where is He now? Is He still there?

SECOND CHILD.

Yes, and He pleads with God in prayer.

FIRST CHILD.

What does He pray for, and for whom?

SECOND CHILD.

He prays that we to Him might come.

FIRST CHILD.

Should we not come? Should we not come?

SECOND CHILD.

Oh, yes! Christ is the sinner's home.

BOTH CHILDREN.

Oh, let us come! oh, let us come!!
Christ is the weary sinner's home."

Extract in "The Twin Brothers.

XLIV.

THE WOMAN WEEPING AT THE TOMB.

WHEN the Son of God came down to be a man, He was killed by wicked men; His friends cried very much when He died. He had one friend called Mary Magdalene: He had been very kind to her. Once seven devils tormented her; Jesus delivered her out of her trouble, and sent the devils away. Ever afterwards Mary loved the Lord, and she listened to His sweet words, and she believed that He was the Son of God. When she saw Him nailed to the cross, she was very unhappy. At last she saw the kind men come and take down His body from the cross, and lay it in a beautiful grave in a garden. This grave was dug out of the side of a rock, and a very great stone was put before it. She went home to make sweet ointment, that she might put it on her dear Lord's body.

One morning she came very early to the

grave with her ointment, and some other women were walking with her. But when she came within sight of the tomb she saw that the great stone was rolled away. Then she thought, 'Some wicked people have rolled away the stone, and have stolen the dead body of my dear Lord!' So she did not go any further, but ran back to the town to ask some good men to come and see what was the matter.

She went to two men who loved Jesus very much; they were called Peter and John.

As soon as they heard what Mary said, they set off running as fast as they could. John ran the fastest, and got first to the grave and looked in; Peter soon came there, too, and he went into it; then John went in too. They saw the linen in which Jesus had been wrapped neatly rolled up, and they saw the cloth which had been bound round His head lying in a place by itself. If wicked men had stolen the body, would they have left the clothes? or, if in a hurry they had left the clothes, would

x

they have left them as Peter and John found them? John now felt sure that Jesus was alive again. I do not know what Peter thought.

Both Peter and John went back to their own home.

But Mary did not go home; she stayed by the tomb all alone, crying very much. Soon she stooped down and looked in. And what did she see? She saw two angels dressed in white; they were sitting on the ground: one was sitting where the bleeding head of Jesus had lain, and the other where His wounded feet had been. Was Mary frightened when she saw the angels? I think she did not know that they were angels, for she was crying very much, and people cannot see clearly when they are crying.

The angels spoke to Mary. Angels speak kindly to every one who loves Jesus.

The angels said, 'Woman, why weepest thou?'

Mary answered, 'Because they have taken away my Lord, and I know not where they have laid Him.'

Then Mary turned round and saw some one else standing near her, but she did not know who it was; she thought it was the gardener.

This man said to her, 'Woman, why weepest thou?'

She answered, 'Sir, if thou hast carried Him away, tell me where thou hast laid Him, that I may take Him away.'

The stranger then spoke one word— 'Mary!'

She knew that voice; it was the Lord who called her by her name. She answered Him by one word—'Master!'

Who can tell what joy she felt at that moment? She wanted to keep her Lord, and not to let Him ever go away. But He said He must soon go up to His Father in heaven. Then He sent a message to all His dear friends, and called them His brothers. This was the message: 'I go up to My Father and to your Father, and to My God and to your God.'

Then Mary went to tell the friends of Jesus that she had seen the Lord, and she told them all He had said to her. Mary was the very first person who saw the Lord after He rose from the grave.

Jesus has been gone into heaven a long while. He is there now. Should you like to see Him in His glory? He will come again. He knows your name. Should you like to hear His voice calling out Mary, or John, or whatever your name may be? Speak to Him now; say, 'Lord Jesus, save me.'

The history of Mary Magdalene is to be found in Luke, viii, 2; John, xx, 1–18.

'Mary to the Saviour's tomb
  Hasted at the early dawn;
Spice she brought, and sweet perfume,
  But the Lord she loved had gone.

For a while she lingering stood,
  Fill'd with sorrow and surprise;
Trembling, while a crystal flood
  Issued from her weeping eyes.

But her sorrows quickly fled
  When she heard His welcome voice:
Christ had risen from the dead,
  Now He bids her heart rejoice.'

XLV.
THE HAPPY MORNING.

THREE women, with jars in their hands, went very quickly along, as if they wished neither to be heard nor seen. They looked as if they had been crying a great deal. What could be the matter? If you could have heard what they said, you might have guessed where they were going. One of the women said to the other, 'Who will roll away the great stone that was put before the tomb?' You see they were going to a tomb. They had lost some dear friend, who was buried in a grave. It must have been a different sort of grave from those in our churchyards, because the graves there are filled up with earth, but this grave had a great stone put before it.

What did these women carry in their hands? Some jars full of very sweet-smelling ointment and spices. That sweet stuff is for the dead body.

Let us watch to see where these women go. It is not to a churchyard, but to a garden. Did you ever see a tomb in a garden? In England the dead are not buried in gardens; but this grave was in a country a great way off. In this garden there was a great rock, and in the side of the rock there was a cave, and there a dead body had been laid, and a stone had been rolled close to the place to stop up the entrance.

When the women came to the garden the sun was rising, and everything was beginning to look bright. They soon caught sight of the rock. How much were they surprised to see the great stone rolled away from before the tomb! Were they glad? Oh, no; they were frightened, for they were afraid that some thieves had been there, and taken away the dead body of their dear friend: so they went into the tomb to look for it; and there they found, not a dead body, but a bright angel. A young man was sitting there, dressed in a long white garment; he was one of those good and beautiful creatures who live with God in heaven. The women were very much afraid when they saw him. But he spoke kindly to them; he said, ' Do not be afraid; you are seeking for Jesus who was crucified; He is not here, for He is risen. Come, see the place where the Lord lay.'

Now, my children, you know who the dear friend was whose body the women were looking for. It was Jesus, the Son of God; He had died three days ago, but God, His Father, had made Him alive again, because He was good. He died to save us from going to hell, but He soon rose out of His grave, for He wished to take us to heaven.

The women were too glad when they heard what the kind angel said; they could hardly believe him, yet they knew he would not tell them lies.

The angel next desired them to tell all the friends of Jesus that He was alive; and then he added, ' You shall see Him.' Oh, what a promise this was! How they did long to see Jesus again!

They ran quickly from the tomb; they were very happy, yet very much afraid: they trembled as they went, but they ran as fast as ever they could, and never stopped to speak to anybody they met on the way. Yet, before they had gone far, they met some one who spoke to them, and they stopped gladly to answer him. They did not expect to see him so soon.

It was Jesus HIMSELF!

The last time they had seen Him He was bleeding, and His hands and feet were pierced with great nails, and His forehead torn with cruel thorns; but now He was quite happy; He would suffer no more, nor weep any more.

When He saw the women, He said, 'Rejoice and be happy.'

They came near Him and held His feet— those feet that had been pierced by nails— the marks were still there; and they worshipped Him as the angels do in heaven, for Jesus is God. Yet still they were frightened

Jesus said, 'Be not afraid; go and tell My brothers that they shall see Me.'

Jesus could not stay with the women; He wanted to see His brothers. These women were His sisters—He called them sisters, because He loved them. Jesus calls all His friends His brothers and sisters. Should you like to be His little brother? Should you like to be His little sister? If you love Him, He reckons you among His brothers and sisters, and He will take you to His Father's house, to be with Him for ever.

This history is written in Matt. xxviii, 1-10; Mark, xvi, 1-8.

THE GRAVE.

' Sweet spices they brought
  On their star-lighted way,
And came to the grave
  By the dawning of day.

" But who will the stone
  From the sepulchre roll!"
They said, as the tears
  From their weeping eyes stole.

The stone is remov'd
  And the Saviour is gone:
Oh, hail, ye disciples,
  This bright Sabbath morn.'

American.

XLVI.

THE HAPPY EVENING.

DID you ever spend a happy evening? But what is a happy evening? No one can be happy who is not wishing and trying to be good. It is children who love God and wish to please Him who are the happy children. When they go and pick flowers in the fields—they feel happy, and when they sit at home and repeat their little hymns to their mothers—they are happy; and even when they are sick and going to die, they are happy, because they know they are going to heaven, that happy place.

I am going now to tell you of some people who loved God very much, and of a very happy evening they spent.

You have heard how the Son of God, Jesus, once lived in this world, and how He was killed by wicked men, and nailed to a cross of wood. Two days after He had

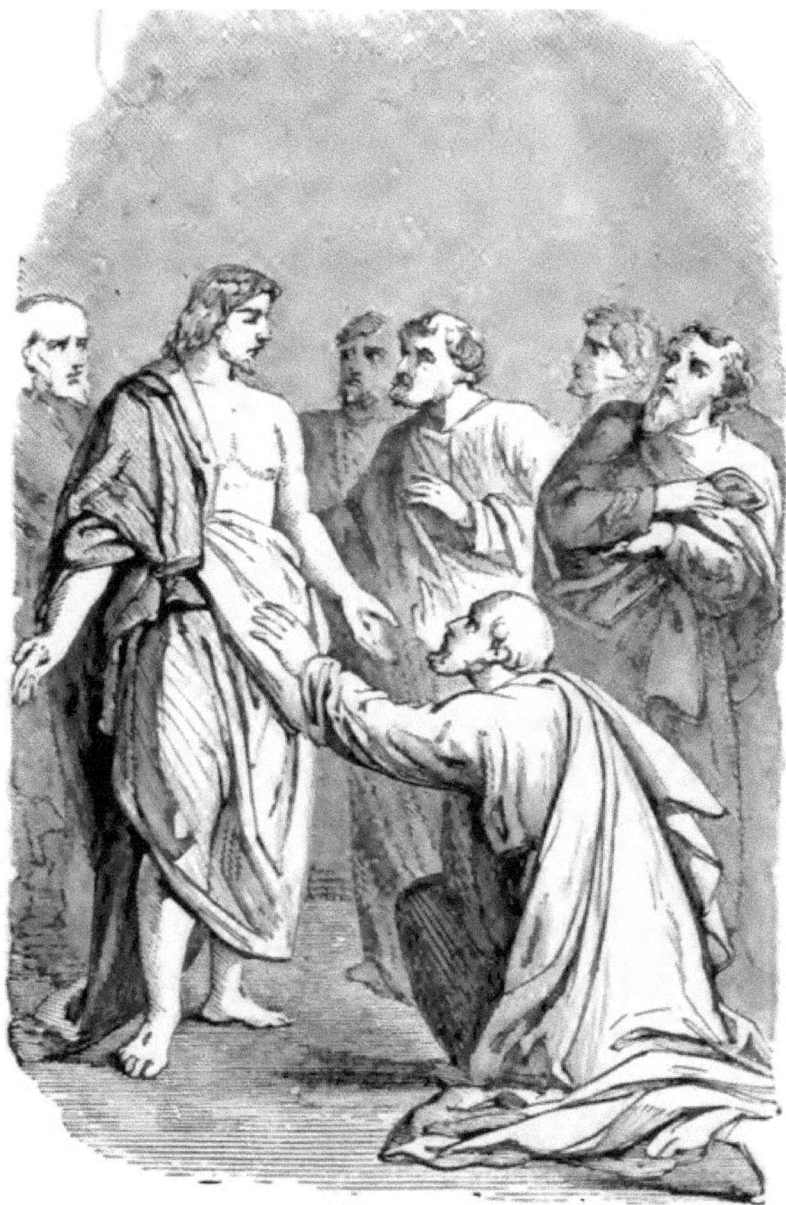

died, some of His friends were in a room together; they were talking about Him. Some of them said to the others, 'We have seen Him; He is alive again.' Others said, 'We have not seen Him.' How much they did wish to see Him! All in a moment — Jesus stood in the midst of the room.

How had He got in? for the doors were locked. He could get in, whether doors were locked or unlocked; it made no difference to Him, for Jesus is God, and can do all things.

Jesus spoke to His friends; these were His words, 'Peace be unto you!' which means, 'Be happy; I will make you happy.'

But though He spoke so sweetly, and looked so kindly at them, His friends were frightened; they thought it could not be Jesus Himself, because they had seen Him die upon the cross: they thought it might be a ghost or spirit, but not the body of their dear Lord.

Jesus knew they were frightened, for He

sees into people's hearts, and knows all they think. So He told them not to be afraid. 'Look at My hands and My feet,' He said; 'see, it is I Myself. A spirit has not flesh and bones as I have.'

Then His friends looked at His hands; they saw the marks of the great nails which had fastened those dear hands to the cross, and when they looked at His feet they saw the marks of the nails in them also. Then they looked at His side, and they saw the deep hole which the spear had made, for a soldier had pierced that tender side with his spear, and made the blood flow out upon the ground. Those marks did not hurt Jesus now; no one could hurt Him now: He never could feel pain again, nor could He die any more.

When His friends had seen those marks, *then* they knew that it was Jesus who spoke to them, and oh, how glad they were! I do not think you were ever so glad in all your life as they were at that minute, for they loved Jesus so very, very much. They knew He had died to save them from going to hell. Oh, how they loved **Him**! Yet still they could hardly believe it was Jesus Himself; it seemed too wonderful that He should be alive again.

Then Jesus said, 'Have you any food here?' He meant to eat something before His friends, to show them He was a real man, and not a ghost or a spirit.

There was a little food in the room; it was the sort of food that poor people generally ate in that country — a piece of broiled fish and a piece of honeycomb. Jesus began to eat this food while all **His** friends looked at Him; then they were sure He was really alive again, and that He was a man like themselves.

But Jesus was God as well as man, and He soon showed them that He was; for He breathed on them, and said, 'Receive ye the Holy Ghost.'

How wonderful this was! His breath was not like our breath. With this breath He gave them the Holy Spirit of God to make them wise and good.

Where is Jesus now? He did not stay

always with His friends in this world; He went up to heaven to His Father; He is with His Father now. But He will come again.

If He were to come into this room this evening should you be glad to see Him? He knows whether you love Him. Do you ever speak to Him now He is in heaven? He hears you when you speak to Him. Do you ever think when you are at play, 'Jesus sees me now; I will not grieve Him by my words?' He knows your thoughts. When He comes again, I hope He will call you by your name, and say, 'Come, come to Me, My child.' He will say to some people, 'Go away!' How dreadful that will be!

You will find this history in Luke. xxiv, 35-43; John, xx, 19-23.

THE DYING YOUTH TO HIS SISTER.

'Sister! I'm weary now;
  Nay, do not, do not weep;
Oh, wipe the death-damp from my brow,
  And let me go to sleep.
There's music ringing in my ear,
  It calls my soul away;
It bids me join that angel-choir.
  Sister! I cannot stay.

Sister! I see them now,
  Bedecked in robes of white,
A glittering crown is on each brow,
  It hath no stain nor blight.
How sweet they strike their golden harps,
  While heaven's high arches ring,
They need no sun nor starry lamps,
  "Jesus, our light," they sing.

Sister! they bid me come,
  I cannot longer stay;
Oh, join me in that blissful home,
  Where tears are wiped away.
Now gently lay my dying head
  Upon thy faithful breast,
Bright angels bend around my bed;
  Sister! I go to rest.'

Children's Friend

XLVII.

CHRIST GOING UP TO HEAVEN.

ONCE the Son of God walked about this world, but He is not here now.

Where is He?

Jesus, the Son of God, is in heaven; He is sitting on the throne of God His Father.

When did He go there? Oh, it is a long while ago since He went up to heaven.

Jesus had been nailed to a cross, and killed, and buried. He had come out of His grave; and the marks of the nails might be seen on His hands and feet. Whenever His friends looked at those marks, they thought of His love in dying for them; for it was for their sins He died; and not for theirs only, but for your sins also, my child.

His friends liked to walk with Him and to talk to Him. About what did Jesus speak? About His Father and about

heaven. He told His friends He should soon leave them, but He made them a promise. What was it? He said that He would send the Holy Spirit down from heaven to be with them.

Who is the Holy Spirit? He is God He comes down and fills the hearts of God's people. It is pleasant to see Jesus, and to walk about with Him, but it is still better to have the Holy Spirit in our hearts, for the Holy Spirit makes people good and happy.

Where was Jesus when He took His last walk with His friends? He was in a town called Jerusalem, and He walked into the country. It was just six weeks since He had been crucified, when He took this walk.

Jesus took His friends by His favourite path; He led them down into a low place over a little stream, then by a garden where olive-trees grew,— then up a green mountain called Olivet.

When they were at the top He began to pray with them. While He prayed, He

lifted up His hands to bless them. In a
moment He was gone—a cloud took Him
up. His friends looked up, and the cloud
was going up higher and higher, till at last
it looked like a speck, and then could not be
seen at all.

But on the mountain-top there stood two
men; they were dressed in white. No one
can tell how bright angels look, or how
sweetly they speak. These angels had
come to comfort the friends of the Lord
Jesus. They said, 'Why do you stand
looking up towards heaven? Jesus shall
come again in the same way that you have
seen Him go into heaven.'

Has Jesus come again? Not yet; but
He will come. Those angels would not
have deceived us; they know that Jesus
will one day come down here again, and
that they shall come with Him. What a
glorious day it will be!

Some people will be very much frightened
when they see Him; they will howl, and
shriek, and try to hide themselves in deep
holes, but they will not be able to get away.

The angels will seize them, and shut them up with Satan.

But some people will be glad to see Jesus; they will say, 'This is our God; we have waited for Him.'

Should you be glad, my dear child, to see Jesus this day? We know not when He will come. Have you prayed to Him to-day? Do you love Him?

But what became of the friends of Jesus, who were standing on Mount Olivet looking up into the sky? They could not stay with the angels, they went back to Jerusalem.

Did they go back crying and sobbing, and saying, 'We have lost our dearest friend?'

Oh, no; they went back quite glad, for they had not lost Jesus; they knew where He was gone; they knew He would pray to His Father, and that He would send down the Holy Spirit very soon.

So they waited at Jerusalem as Jesus had told them, and in ten days Jesus did

send down the Holy Spirit upon His dear
friends.

There is a sweet name given to the Holy
Spirit; it is this—the Comforter. Why is
He called the Comforter? Because He
comforts people when they are in trouble.
When we are unhappy we like to be comforted. If a little child falls down and
hurts itself, it runs crying to its mother;
it wants to be comforted. And oh, how
tenderly a mother comforts her little darling! She takes it on her knee and kisses
it, and says, 'Tell mother what is the matter. Has it hurt its dear little hand?' And
then she kisses the hand—the child leaves
off crying, and leans its head upon its mother's
bosom.

But no mother can comfort as the Holy
Spirit can. He tells people that God loves
them, and has forgiven their sins, and will
take them to heaven. My child, ask God
for His Holy Spirit, and He will hear you.

You may find the history of Jesus going
up to heaven in Luke, xxiv, 50 to end ·
Acts, i, 1–12.

JESUS DIED FOR ME.

'I love to sing of that great Power
 That made the earth and sea;
But better still I love the song
 Of "Jesus died for me."

I love to sing of shrub and flower.
 Of field, and plant, and tree:
My sweetest note for ever is,
 That "Jesus died for me."

I love to hear the little birds
 Attune their notes with glee;
But larks and linnets never heard
 That "Jesus died for me."

I love to think of angels' songs,
 From sin and sorrow free;
But angels cannot strike their notes
 To "Jesus died for me."

I love to know the time shall come
 When man shall happy be;
But I am happy *now*, because
 My "Jesus died for me."

And when I reach that happy place.
 From all temptation free,
I 'll swell the everlasting choir
 With "Jesus died for me."'

XLVIII.

THE HOLY SPIRIT COMING DOWN FROM HEAVEN.

EVERY one likes to hear good news. If a person comes into a room and says, 'I have some good news to tell you,' every one looks up and says, 'Do tell us.'

What was the best news ever told to people in this world? It was this—'Jesus has died to save you.' Who told this news first? It was the twelve apostles. They were twelve friends who walked about with Jesus, the Son of God, when He was in this world; they saw Him nailed to the cross, they saw Him after He rose out of His grave, and they saw Him go up to heaven in the clouds.

Before Jesus went up, He said to them, 'Go, and tell good news to every creature.'

What good news? That Jesus had died to save sinners.

But how could the apostles tell this good

news to every creature? There are a great many different languages in the world; some people speak English, and some French, and some Italian, and some German. The apostles did not know all the languages; they knew only their own language, which was the Jewish language; but Jesus could make them know every language. Before He went up into heaven, He told them He would send down the Holy Spirit to help them to preach the good news.

Who is the Holy Spirit? He is God. In heaven there are the Father, the Son, and the Spirit; these three are one God;—one is not greater than the other; they are three in one, and one in three. This is a great wonder which nobody can understand, but we may be sure it is true, for God has said it. It was the Father who sent His Son to die for the world; it was the Son who died upon the cross; and it is the Holy Spirit who comes into people's hearts, and makes them good, and wise, and happy.

After Jesus was gone up into heaven the twelve apostles lived in a city called Jerusalem, in a large room upstairs. A great many people who loved Jesus used to come very often and pray with them. Some of these were women, and one of them was Mary, the mother of Jesus.

Ten days passed away, and then a very wonderful thing happened. It was in the morning, before nine o'clock. The apostles and their friends were praying together in that large room, when suddenly a great noise was heard from heaven. It was like the noise of the wind when it blows very hard, and this sound filled the whole house where the apostles were sitting.

But there was not only a noise, there was a wonderful sight too. There were seen flames of fire in the shape of tongues. They came and sat upon all the people in the room.

Immediately those people were filled with the Holy Spirit, and they began to speak in different languages which they had never learned.

What did they speak about ? They **gave** the message which Jesus had told them to give—'**Jesus died to save** sinners.' They did not stay in the room upstairs, but went into the street, that every one might hear them.

At that time there were in Jerusalem a great many people from other countries, for it was a great day among the Jews, and those Jews who lived in distant places came to Jerusalem to worship God on that day. How much surprised they were to hear people, **who had** never learned, speaking so many **different** languages !

Some wicked people were there who **said** 'These men are drunk.' I suppose **they** did not understand the strange languages, and thought the apostles **were** talking non-sense.

Soon there **was** a great crowd in the streets of Jerusalem ; they were saying to one another, ' What can this be ? '

Then **one** of the apostles, named **Peter,** stood **up** to preach.

This was the first sermon that was preached

after Jesus had gone up to heaven. The crowd listened to it very attentively.

What was it about?

It was about Jesus.

Peter told the crowd that the man who had been nailed to the cross a little while ago was the Son of God, and that He had sent down His Holy Spirit from heaven. Peter said, 'You were so wicked as to kill Him, but God His Father has raised Him out of His grave, and taken Him to heaven. He is now your King, and He has sent down the Holy Spirit.'

When the people heard that they had crucified the Son of God, many of them were very unhappy; they remembered how He had been treated—how He had been spit upon and crowned with thorns; how His back had been torn with the scourge, and His hands with the nails; they remembered how they had laughed at Him as He was dying, and how meekly He had borne all their jeers. No wonder they were unhappy now.

Three thousand people came to the

apostles and said, 'What shall we do?'
Then Peter said, 'Repent.' He told them
Jesus would forgive them, and he said he
would baptize them, or wash them in water,
as a sign that Jesus had washed away their
sins with His blood, and that God would
give them the Holy Spirit.

How happy the men were to think that
Jesus would forgive all their wickedness!
What a comfort that was!

You may read this history in Acts, ii.

COME.

'There's a voice that sweetly calleth,
   Little children, come away,
While your life is bright and sunny,
   In the morning of your day.
Come to Jesus; He will fold you
   Closely to His tender breast,
In the hour of danger hold you,
   Give you happiness and rest.

When at night you shut your eyelids
   Tightly o'er the sleepy eyes,
Angel-watchers round your pillow
   He will send you from the skies.
When the night of pain and sickness,
   Or the clouds of death draw near,
He will save your heart from sadness,
   And your parting soul from fear.'

XLIX.

THE TWO LIARS.

Do you know who is the father of lies? It is a creature called Satan. He was once a bright angel in heaven, but a long while ago he grew wicked, and God cast him down into darkness. But he comes here and teaches people to tell lies, even children.

Satan told the first lie that ever was told in this world. He told it to the first woman whom God had made. Her name was Eve. God had told Eve that if she ate the fruit of a certain tree she should die, and Satan said she should *not* die. That was the lie.

Now I am going to tell you of two liars who lived a long while after Jesus was gone up to heaven. They were a husband and a wife. The name of the man was Ananias, and the name of the woman was Sapphira. They agreed together to tell a lie.

It was this.

Z

They had a piece of land, and they sold it for some money; then they said to each other, 'Let us take *some* of the money and give it to a good minister called Peter, and tell him to give it the poor.'

Was not this very good of them? Yes, it *seems* good; but now hear what they meant to say.

'Let us make Peter *think* that we have given *all* the money we got for the land to the poor.'

You know this was not true.

They wanted to *seem* very good and generous, but they did not like to part with *all* their money: so they made up their minds to tell this untruth. They might have kept *all* their money, but why tell a lie?

Ananias went with *part* of the money to Peter, and gave it him for the poor. But Peter knew that he meant to deceive him, and he said to Ananias, 'Why has Satan filled your heart to tell this lie? You need not have sold the land; you need not have given away the money. You have lied unto God.'

As soon as Ananias heard these words he dropped down DEAD.

Every one who heard of his death was very much afraid, for they knew he had been struck dead by God for telling a lie. Some young men came and wrapped him in a cloth, and carried him out and buried him.

His wife Sapphira did not hear what had happened to her husband. About three hours after his death she came into the house where Peter was. Then Peter asked her for how much she had sold the land. And she said she had sold it for less than she really had, in hopes of making Peter think that she had given away *all* the money.

As soon as she had said this, Peter said, 'How is it that ye have agreed together to tempt the Spirit of the Lord? Behold, the feet of them which have buried thy husband are at the door, and shall carry thee out.'

Immediately she fell down at Peter's feet and died, and the young men came in and found her dead, and carried her out, and buried her by her husband. So in one day these two liars died and were buried.

If God were to strike all liars dead, how many sudden deaths would take place! But God is very patient, and bears with sinners a long while, that they may have time to repent, and to ask for pardon. For God will pardon sinners if they ask Him. Yes, He will pardon all who wish to leave off telling lies. The reason why He is so ready to pardon is, because He is kind and merciful, and because He gave His only Son Jesus Christ to die upon the cross to save sinners from being punished.

But there is a place to which all liars who are not pardoned will be sent one day. It is not a lake of water, but a lake of fire. Satan, the father of lies, will be cast into it, and all his children. These are the words of God: 'All liars shall have their part in the lake which burneth with fire and brimstone.' (Rev. xxi, 8.)

You can read about those two liars, Ananias and Sapphira, in Acts, v, 1–11.

GOD HATES SIN.

‘ Have we not known, nor heard, nor read
    How God abhors deceit and wrong?
How Ananias was struck dead,
    Caught with a lie upon his tongue ?

So did his wife Sapphira die,
    When she came in and grew so bold
As to confirm the wicked lie
    That just before her husband told.

The Lord delights in them that speak
    The words of truth; but every liar
Must have his portion in the lake
    That burns with brimstone and with fire.’

DR. WATTS.

GOD FORGIVES SIN.

‘ Here’s a message of love
    Come down from above,
To invite little children to Heaven;
    In God’s blessed book
    Poor sinners may look,
And see how all sin is forgiven.
    And then when they die
    He takes them on high,
To be with Him in Heaven above;
    For so kind is His heart,
    That He never will part
From a child that has tasted His love.’

Dublin Farthing Hymn-Book.

L.

THE MAN IN THE CHARIOT.

AFTER Jesus was gone up into heaven, there lived a good man named Philip. An angel once spoke to him, and told him to go into a desert place.

Why did the angel desire Philip to go to a desert? You will soon see the reason.

When Philip got to the desert, he saw a chariot passing along. In this chariot a very rich man was riding. The Spirit of God said to Philip, 'Go up to that chariot.' So Philip went close up to it. There was a very dark man, almost black, sitting in the chariot, reading out aloud. The carriage went so slowly and so softly over the sand that Philip could hear what the man was reading.

Philip listened, and he heard the words, 'He was led as a lamb to the slaughter; and like a lamb dumb before his shearer, so He opened not His mouth.

Philip knew that these words were in the Bible, and he understood what they meant, but he thought that the rich man did not understand; so he said to him, 'Understandest thou what thou readest?' The rich man answered, 'How can I understand except some one explain it to me?'

You see that the rich man was not proud. A proud person is ashamed to say he does not understand; a proud person does not like to be taught. But this rich man wished Philip to teach him, and he asked him to come up and sit in the chariot by his side.

As soon as Philip was seated in the carriage, the rich man said to him, 'I do not know who is spoken of in the verse I have been reading. Who is the lamb led to the slaughter?'

Then Philip told the rich man who that meek lamb was. How many little English children know who that lamb was! Jesus was the Lamb of God who was nailed to the cross for our sins, and like a lamb, when the shearer is shearing him, so He

was gentle and quiet while the wicked people were tormenting **Him.**

Philip told the rich man a great deal about Jesus. **He told** him, also, that people who believed in Jesus were baptized, or washed in water, **as a** sign that their sins were washed **away in the blood** of Christ.

When the rich man heard Philip say this, he wished very much to be baptized.

At last he **saw** some water. There is not much water in the desert, but now **and** then there **is** a little pool or a narrow stream to be seen.

The rich man was glad to see the water, and he cried out, 'Here is water. Why cannot I be baptized?'

Then Philip said, 'If thou believest with all thine heart, thou mayest.'

The rich man replied, 'I believe **that** Jesus Christ is the Son of God.'

Then the rich man desired the driver to stop the carriage, and he got out, and so did Philip, and they went down into the water, and Philip baptized the rich man.

Did Philip get into the carriage again, and go home with his new friend?

No; the Spirit of God caught him away, and put him down in a town a great way off.

How much surprised the rich man must have been to find that Philip was gone away so suddenly! But he was not unhappy. Now he could understand the Bible; now he believed in Jesus; now he was baptized in His name, and he was a true Christian. He knew that Jesus loved him, and would take him to live with Him for ever. Could he be unhappy? He got into his chariot again full of joy, and he went back to his own country. It was a heathen country, where people worshipped idols. But soon the people turned from idols to serve the living and true God.

Do you think the rich man often read over that verse, 'He was led as a lamb to the slaughter?' This was the first verse about the Lord Jesus that he ever knew. Is there any verse that you are very fond of? Perhaps you learned some little verse

a long while ago about Christ that you will
never forget.

If you want to find the verse about the
lamb, look for Isa. liii, 7. If you want to
read more about this rich man, look for
Acts, viii, 26 to the end.

THE LOVING SAVIOUR.

' How loving is Jesus
 Who came from the sky,
 In tenderest pity
 For sinners to die!
His hands and His feet were nail'd to the tree,
And all this He suffer'd for you and for me.

 How gladly does Jesus
 Free pardon impart,
 To all who receive Him
 By faith in their heart!
No evil befalls them, their home is above,
And Jesus throws round them the arms of His love.

 Oh, give, then, to Jesus
 Your earliest days;
 They only are blessed
 Who walk in His ways;
In life and in death He will still be your friend,
For whom Jesus loves, He loves to the end.'

Writer unknown.

LI.

THE MAN WHO SAW THE GREAT LIGHT.

SAUL was once a very wicked man. He lived in the world soon after Jesus had been crucified, and after He had gone to sit on His Father's throne in heaven. Saul had never seen Jesus, he had only heard of Him. He did not believe that He was the Son of God, and he hated all those people who did believe in Him. Saul was a very cruel man; he went about from one city to another to get hold of good people, and to put them in prison.

At last he set out on a journey to a city called Damascus. Why did he go there? To put in prison those who loved the Lord Jesus. He did not go alone; some men went with him to help him.

It was about twelve o'clock in the middle of the day, when he came near Damascus. The sun was shining bright; when sud-

denly a greater light than the sun was seen in the sky. It was so great a light that Saul could not bear to look at it; he fell to the ground, and the men that were with him—they also fell to the ground

While they were all lying on their faces very much frightened, Saul heard a voice speaking from the sky. No one heard it but Saul.

Whose voice was it? It was a voice that you have never heard, but you will hear it one day. It was the voice of the Lord Jesus Christ.

And what did Jesus say? He said, 'Saul, Saul, why persecutest thou Me?'

What did He mean by these words? He meant that He was grieved because Saul tried to hurt His people; for Jesus loves His people very much indeed.

Did Saul answer the Lord Jesus?

Yes, he did; he said, 'Who art Thou, Lord?'

Then the Lord said, 'I am Jesus whom thou persecutest; it is hard for thee to kick against the pricks.' While Saul had been trying to hurt good people, he had only been hurting himself. He had been like a child kicking against spikes, who hurts his own little feet, and makes them bleed.

All this time Saul was very much frightened; he was now sorry for his wickedness. and he said to the Lord, 'What wilt Thou have me to do?'

Then the Lord said, 'Arise, go into the city, and it shall be told thee what thou shalt do.'

When Saul got up from the ground, he found that he was blind—the great light had put out his eyes.

The other men were not blind, and they led him by the hand into Damascus, and took him to a lodging in a street called Straight Street. There he stayed very unhappy, thinking of his sins, and of the Lord Jesus Christ.

Soon God sent a good man to comfort him. This man was called Ananias, and he spoke kindly to Saul, and put his hands on him, and said, 'Brother Saul, receive

thy sight.' Immediately Saul was able to
see. Then he was baptized, and afterwards
he took some food, and began to feel
stronger.

Ananias told Saul what the Lord wished
him to do. What was it? To preach
about Jesus; to tell everybody that He
had been crucified for their sins, and that
He was ready to forgive them, and that He
was sitting at the right hand of the Father,
and that He would come again to judge the
world.

And did Saul do what the Lord commanded? Oh, yes; he spent the rest of his
days in preaching about Jesus.

He did not preach to the Jews only, but
he went to far countries, where people
worshipped idols, and he told them of the
true God, and of His Son Jesus Christ
And multitudes of people turned unto the
Lord.

Wicked people hurt *him*, as *he* had once
hurt good people. Once they threw great
stones at him, till he seemed to be dead,
and eight times they beat him in a cruel

manner. Often they put him in prison, and at last they cut off his head.

Saul is now called *Paul*. He had two names. When he was alive some people called him Saul, and some called him Paul. *Now* he is dead, everybody calls him Paul. He wrote a great many beautiful letters, and they are printed in the Bible. Children cannot understand all these letters, but they can understand part. Here is a **verse** which Paul wrote that you can understand: 'Christ Jesus came into the world to save sinners, of whom I am the chief.' (1 Tim. i, 15.)

You will find the history of Paul seeing the light in Acts, ix, 1–22; xxii, 1–21; xxvi, 1–20.

THE STRAY LAMB.

Upon a rugged mountain,
  Whose top was white with snow,
And over which the storm-clouds hung
  Very black and low,
A little lamb had wander'd,
  And knew not where to go.

The ground was hard and stony,
  And hurt its tender feet;
The grass was very scanty,
  And scarcely fit to eat.
Nor was there any water
  That tasted good and sweet.

The shepherd heard its bleating,
  And pitied its distress!
He could not bear to leave it
  In all its loneliness;
And so he went to find it,
  And thus its woes redress.

But, oh! would you believe it?
  The little foolish thing
Refus'd the kindly succour
  The shepherd came to bring,
And to that dreary mountain
  Perversely chose to cling.

The shepherd would have carried it
  Rejoicing to his fold;
He would have fed it daily,
  And have shelter'd it from cold;
He would have kept it safely
  From lions fierce and bold.

How strange to be unwilling
  With such a friend to go!
And yet, dear little children,
  Have you not acted so?
When Christ has gently call'd you,
  Your heart has answer'd " No."

He left His throne of glory
  To seek such lambs as you;
For that you far had wander'd,
  From Him the Saviour knew:
And, oh! He long'd to save you,
  And make you happy too.

Then do not grieve that Saviour,
  Nor from Him turn away;
Why should you any longer
  In sin or folly stray?
Let the Good Shepherd bring you
  Within His fold to-day.

How full of joy and gladness,
  The little lambs are there!
No foe can ever harm them
  While in their Saviour's care;
And Jesus gently leads them,
  In pastures green and fair.'

Early Days.

LII.

THE MAN WHO SAW HEAVEN BEFORE HE DIED.

WHEN the Son of God lived down in this world He had many friends. His dearest friend was called John; John was a poor fisherman, but he left his boat and his nets that he might go about with Jesus from place to place, and hear His sweet words.

At last the time came when Jesus must leave His dear friends. The evening before He died, He took supper with twelve of His friends. It was the custom in that country for people to lie down at supper to rest themselves. John lay down next to Jesus, and leaned his head upon his Lord's bosom. Was it not pleasant to be so near the Son of God?

That night Jesus went into a garden to pray, and John went with Him, and so did the other friends—all but one, who did not really love his Lord. Some wicked men came to the garden and bound Jesus with ropes, and led Him away. John was afraid of going with his Lord; he left Him, and went a good way off. But afterwards he went to look for Him; he saw Him hanging upon His cross of wood, with nails through His hands and feet. John stood near the cross, and next to John stood Mary, the mother of Jesus. Jesus loved His mother; He looked at her and then at John, and He said to her, 'Behold thy son!' And He said to John, 'Behold thy mother!' John understood what his Lord meant, and very soon afterwards he took the poor mother to his own home.

John saw his Lord die upon the cross that day at three o'clock, and he saw the soldiers come to see whether He was dead, and he saw one of them thrust a spear into the side of Jesus. The spear did not hurt Him, because He was dead, but from His side—blood and water came flowing out. It was very strange to see water as well as blood.

It is the precious blood of Jesus that washes away sin. Water can make your body clean, but the blood of Jesus can make your heart clean. Jesus died to take away our sins.

John was **very** unhappy when Jesus was dead, and he shed tears of sorrow.

But in three days Jesus was alive again. A woman came one morning to tell John that Jesus **was** alive, and John ran very fast to His grave to see whether it was true. Peter ran with him. John got to the grave **first**, and looked in. When Peter got there he went in. After Peter had gone in, John went in too, and he saw the white linen clothes that had been wrapped round Jesus lying in the grave. Then John believed that his Lord was really alive.

That very evening John saw his dear Lord again. How much pleased He was to see Him all at once standing in the room!

He saw Him again another day by the waterside.

Another **day** he walked with Him up a high hill; he heard Him pray, and suddenly he saw a cloud come and take Him up into heaven. John could not go up in the cloud with Him; he stayed down in this world and told everybody about Jesus, and about how He died upon the cross to take away our sins.

Did John ever see his Lord again? Yes. When he was a very old man John was sent to a place called Patmos. It was a piece of land with water all round it, and a great many wicked people were sent to this land as a punishment for their crimes. But had John done some wicked thing? No; he had not stolen, nor killed any one; he had preached about Jesus, and a cruel king sent him to this place as a punishment.

One day (it was Sunday) he heard a voice behind him like the sound of a trumpet, and he turned to see who it was, and he saw Jesus—not looking as He once had done, but shining very bright—yes, as bright as the sun shines at noon. John was so much surprised, that he fell at the feet of Jesus, as if he had been dead. But Jesus touched him with His right hand,

and said, 'Fear not; I am the first and
the last. I am He that liveth and was
dead, and, behold, I am alive for evermore!'
Then Jesus talked to him, and told him to
write down what He said in a book; and
John did write it, and you may read what
Jesus said to him.

Afterwards John saw the angels in heaven, and saw people who once lived in this
world, all clothed in white, and looking so
happy, and singing so sweetly, and he saw
Jesus sitting on His throne with God His
Father. It was an angel who showed him
all the beautiful sights in heaven.

John was so much pleased with what he
saw, that he was going to worship the angel;
but the angel said, 'See thou do it not:
worship God.' We must not even worship
angels, because they are only creatures
whom God made.

Jesus spoke again to John, and told him
that He would open the gates of heaven to
let in people who do His commandments.

Those are the people who are washed in
the blood of the Lamb.

But Jesus will not open the gates to those who do not believe — nor to those who tell lies. 'All liars shall have their part in the lake which burneth with fire and brimstone'   •

Jesus will come again to this world. He said to John, 'Behold, I come quickly.' And John said, 'Come, Lord Jesus.' He has not come yet. John has been dead a long while; his spirit is in heaven with Jesus.

Do you wish to live with Jesus? Ask Jesus to wash away your sins in His blood; He has forgiven a great many sinners, and I know He will forgive you. There are many now singing glory in heaven unto Him that loved them, and washed them from their sins in His own blood. (Rev. i, 5.)

THE ANGELS.

' I want to be an angel,
   And with the angels stand,
A crown upon my forehead,
   A harp within my hand;
There right before my Saviour,
   So glorious and so bright,
I 'd wake the sweetest music,
   And praise Him day and night.

I never should be weary,
   Nor ever shed a tear,
Nor ever know a sorrow,
   Nor ever feel a fear;
But blessed, pure, and holy,
   I 'd dwell in Jesus' sight,
And with ten thousand thousands,
   Praise Him both day and night.

I know I'm weak and sinful,
   But Jesus will forgive;
For many little children
   Have gone to heaven to live.
Dear Saviour, when I languish,
   And lay me down to die,
Oh, send a shining angel,
   To bear me to the sky.'

Writer unknown.

A LITTLE SISTER'S DREAM

'I had a dream, my brother dear,
  Whilst fast asleep last night·
I thought I was in heaven's courts,
  And rob'd in spotless white:

A crown of gold was on my head,
  A palm was in my hand,
And I had join'd the multitude
  Who tread that happy land.

I saw the shining throng of saints,
  The elders, twenty-four,
Who round about the Saviour's throne
  Their ceaseless praises pour.

And when I woke, myself to find
  A pilgrim still below,
I thought how happy we should be
  If you and I could go.

For ever to that happy land,
  Where sorrow is not known;
Where only they who do His will
  Can go, and they alone.'

H. WELLS. in ' Early Days

QUESTIONS ON THE CHAPTERS.

I.

Who made the world ?
Where does God live ?
Are all angels good ?
What are wicked angels called ?
How did God make the world ?
What shape is the world ?
How did God make man's body ?
How did God make man's soul ?
What did God call the first man ?
How did God make the woman ?
Why cannot dogs think about God ?
May children speak to God ?

II.

When do children begin to do wrong ?
How do some children try to hide their naughtiness ?

Where did Adam and Eve live?

Who did not like to see Adam and Eve happy?

Why is the devil called the old serpent?

What did Adam and Eve do when they heard God's voice in the garden?

What excuse did Adam make?

What excuse did Eve make?

What did God do to the serpent?

How did God show His love to Adam and Eve?

III.

Who committed the first murder?

What made Abel love God?

Why was Cain angry?

What did God say to Cain?

Did Cain mind what God said?

What did Cain do to Abel one day?

Why did Cain think he could hide his sin?

What did God ask Cain?

What lie did Cain tell?

What punishment did God give Cain?

How will God punish liars and murderers?

Who was the first man who went to heaven?

IV.

How many years is it since the world was drowned?

What sort of people lived in the world then?

What did God tell Noah to do?

How many rooms were there in the ark?

Who were to go into the ark?

Who shut the door of the ark?

How long did it rain?

How did Noah know when the world was dry?

What did God promise Noah?

What beautiful sign did God give him?

What will happen to the world some day?

Who will be saved then?

V.

What did God say to the people of Israel?

What were the Israelites afraid of?

What did the people beg Moses to do for them?

Where did Moses go ?

What did Moses bring down ?

Who minded all God's laws ?

Why was the Son of God punished ?

For whose sake must we ask God to forgive us ?

How many laws are there ?

VI.

What does God do for us whilst we sleep ?

Who makes bread ?

Who makes corn ?

Why did God once send the Israelites no rain ?

What good man lived in Israel then ?

How did God feed Elijah ?

What wonderful thing happened to Elijah at last ?

Why is God kind to sinners ?

What promise has God made for the time of famine ?

VII.

What did a great king once set up?

What did he command every one to do when they heard the music?

Who refused to bow down?

How did the king punish them?

What happened to the soldiers?

Who walked with the Jews in the fire?

What did the king call out to the Jews?

How did the king say he would punish people who spoke against the God of the Jews?

VIII.

Why was a good man shut up with lions?

What sly plan did the lords make?

Did Daniel leave off praying?

Who told the king they had seen him pray?

Could the king change his law?

How did the king comfort Daniel?

Could Daniel get out of the den?

What did the king say in the morning?

What was done to the wicked lords?

Who goes about like a lion ?

Who can keep him from hurting us ?

IX.

Who saw a bright angel ?

What was the angel's name ?

What did Gabriel say to Mary ?

What was to be her baby's name ?

Why would God send His Son ?

Did Mary believe what Gabriel told her ?

Where was the baby born ?

What was the baby's cradle ?

Did the people in the inn know who the baby was ?

How can you be blessed like Mary ?

What does Jesus call people who try to please Him ?

X.

What wonderful thing happened to some shepherds one night ?

What did the angel tell them ?

When the angel had done speaking, what did the shepherds see and hear ?

What did the shepherds do?

Where did the shepherds find the baby?

Will the shepherds see him again?

Who fetches the souls of children who love Jesus?

XI.

What was the name of Mary's husband?

How old was her baby when Mary took him to Jerusalem?

Why did Mary take her baby to the Temple?

Who came into the Temple?

What had God promised Simeon?

What did Simeon say when he had seen the babe?

What did Simeon call the babe?

Who was Anna?

How old was she?

Did any one hear Anna praise God?

When may we see the Son of God?

XII.

What made the wise men come to Jerusalem?

Who was king at Jerusalem?

What did the wise men wish to find out?

Who told the wise men to go to Bethlehem?

What did the wise men do when they saw the babe?

Why did they not go back to Jerusalem?

Why did Herod kill the babies?

Where did God desire Joseph to go with Mary and her babe?

Who is the king of the Jews?

XIII.

What sort of boy was the Lord Jesus?

Who was His father?

Where did Jesus go when He was twelve years old?

What did Joseph and Mary do when they could not find Jesus?

Where did they find Him at last?

What did they say to Him?

What did Jesus answer?

How can you be like Jesus?

XIV.

Where did John preach?

What did John say to the people?

What did John do to the people who were sorry for their sins?

What wonderful thing happened when Jesus was baptized?

Who is like a dove?

What would make you happy?

XV.

Who teaches people to be wicked?

What sort of hearts have we got?

Could Satan make Jesus wicked?

Where did Jesus spend forty days?

Did Satan know Jesus was hungry?

What did he ask Him to do?

Why did Satan take Jesus to the top of a very high place?

What did Jesus see when He was on the mountain?

What did Satan promise to do, if Jesus would worship him?

Who came to the Lord Jesus when Satan was
gone ?

XVI.

When John saw Jesus, what did he call Him ?
How is Jesus like a lamb ?
Who told Simon about Jesus ?
What new name did Jesus give him ?
What does Peter mean ?
How can you be like Peter ?

XVII.

What promise did Nathaniel and Philip find
in the Bible ?
Which of them found Jesus first ?
What did Jesus say when He saw Nathaniel
coming ?
Where did Jesus say Nathaniel had been ?
What made Nathaniel sure that Jesus is the
Son of God ?

XVIII.

What did the traveller ask the woman to give
Him ?

Why did she refuse ?

What did the woman **ask the traveller to give**
her ?

What did she do when she found **out who He**
was ?

What makes people happy ?

What must you pray **for** ?

XIX.

Who was a friend of the fishermen ?

Why did Jesus get into **the** ship ?

Who were with Him in the ship ?

What miracle did Jesus do for the fishermen ?

What prayer did Simon Peter make ?

What promise did Jesus give him ?

XX.

What did Jesus say to the poor widow ?

What did He say to the young man ?

Why did Jesus die ?

Who **will** judge the dead ?

XXI.

What sort of people loved Jesus?
What sort of people did not love Him?
How did the poor woman show her love?
Why did not Simon love Jesus?
What did Jesus say to the poor woman?

XXII.

Who made a poor man miserable?
What did Jesus say to the devils?
What did the devils ask Jesus?
What did the foolish people ask Jesus?
What did the poor man ask Jesus?
What may you ask Jesus?

XXIII.

Why did Jairus beg Jesus to come to his
house?

What bad news did Jairus hear on the way?

Which of the disciples went into the house
with Jesus?

Why did the people laugh at what Jesus said?

What did Jesus say to the girl?

What will Jesus say one day to all the dead?

XXIV.

What was the name of Salome's uncle?

How did Salome please him?

What was the name of Salome's mother?

What did Herodias tell Salome to ask for?

Why did Herod grant this wicked request?

What became of John's body?

XXV.

How many people did Jesus feed?

Had the disciples any food with them?

Was there food enough for all?

What does Jesus call children who love Him?

XXVI.

Who is the best friend we can have when we are in trouble?

Did Jesus go with His disciples in the boat?

What did they see in the night?

Why were they frightened?

What did Peter wish to do?

What is trusting in God called?

What happened when Jesus got into a ship?

XXVII.

What did a poor mother call Jesus?

What was the promise God made to David?

How did Jesus treat the poor woman at first?

Why did He keep her waiting?

What sweet answer did she make to Him?

When did her daughter get well?

What words would the happy mother never forget?

XXVIII.

Who went up the mountain with Jesus?

What two men did they see with Jesus?

What did the men talk about with Jesus?

What did Peter wish to do?

What did the voice from Heaven say?

When might the disciples tell what they had seen?

XXIX.

Who had asked the nine disciples for help while Jesus was away?

Could they help him?

When the poor father saw Jesus coming, what did he do?

Was he quite sure Jesus could help him?

What right prayer did he make?

How did Jesus cast out the devil?

Why could not the disciples cast him out?

XXX.

Where did Martha and Mary live?

What visitor came one day to see them?

What did Martha do when He came?

Where did Mary like to sit?

How did Jesus answer Martha when she complained?

If you love Jesus, what will you do?

XXXI.

How ought we to feel when we see cripples?

Where did Jesus see a poor cripple?

What did He say to her?

What did she do when she was cured?

Who was angry with Jesus for working this great miracle?

What name did Jesus call him?

XXXII.

How did Jesus cure a blind beggar in Jerusalem?

What did the beggar tell people who asked him about his being cured?

How did the wicked men behave to this poor beggar now he was cured?

When Jesus found him, what question did He ask him?

What will be sure to make us happy?

XXXIII.

How did Jesus treat children when He was on earth ?

Why did Jesus once take a child in His arms ? ·

When mothers brought children to Jesus, what did the disciples tell them to do ?

What did Jesus say about the little children ?

How did children once please Jesus in the Temple ?

Who did not like to hear their sweet voices ?

What words of David did Jesus repeat to these wicked men ?

XXXIV.

What is a leper ?

Why were there ten lepers together ?

What did they call out to Jesus ?

What did Jesus tell them to do ?

When were they cured ?

What did the lepers do when they found they were cured ?

C C

How many thanked Jesus?

Of what nation was the thankful leper?

XXXV.

What did a blind man hear as he sat by the roadside?

What did he cry out?

Why did he go on crying out, when at first Jesus did not listen to him?

What question did Jesus ask him?

What was his answer?

Did Jesus hear his prayer, and cure him?

How ought we to pray?

XXXVI.

Who climbed into a sycomore tree when Jesus was passing?

Why did Zaccheus climb up into the tree?

What did Jesus say to him as He looked up at him in the tree?

What was Zaccheus's business?

How did Zaccheus show he was sorry for having cheated people?

What sweet words of comfort did Jesus say to nim ?

XXXVII.

Where did Jesus often go with His disciples?

The last time He went, which of His disciples did not go with Him ?

Why was Jesus sad ?

Which of the disciples did He take with Him into the garden ?

What prayer did Jesus make ?

What did He mean by the cup ?

How often did Jesus go alone to pray ?

Who came to comfort Him ?

What sad sight did the angel behold ?

What were the three disciples doing ?

Who showed the wicked men the way into the garden ?

XXXVIII.

When Peter heard how Jesus was going to suffer, what did he think he could do ?

What did Jesus say he would do ?

Why did Peter deny Jesus ?

What was it made Peter sorry for his sin ?

After Jesus rose from the grave, what question did He ask Peter three times?

When ought we to feel very unhappy?

XXXIX.

Did Jesus know how wicked Judas was?

Did the other disciples know it?

Why was Judas angry when Mary poured the ointment on Jesus' feet?

What promise did Judas make to the wicked men?

How much did they agree to give him?

Was Judas at the last supper?

What did Jesus say to him just before he left the room?

How did Judas show the wicked men which was Jesus?

What did Judas do with the silver?

How did Judas die?

XL.

What was the name of the judge before whom Jesus was brought?

How did Pilate try to save Jesus from the wicked men?

Who sent a message to Pilate to beg him not to hurt Him?

Why did Pilate wash his hands?

What was done to Jesus before He was crucified?

How did the soldiers treat Him?

XLL

What o'clock was it when Jesus was nailed on the cross?

What prayer did He make to His Father?

What did the soldiers do with His clothes?

What great wonder happened at twelve o'clock?

How long did Jesus hang on the cross?

What did the soldier give Him to drink when He was thirsty?

What happened when Jesus died?

XLII.

Who were crucified with Jesus?

What was the difference between the two thieves?

How did one of the thieves show he was sorry?

What sweet promise did Jesus make him?

What did the soldiers do to the thieves?

XLIII.

Who asked for the body of Jesus?

Who went with Joseph?

Where did they put the body of the Lord?

Why could not Jesus' body corrupt or turn to dust?

Why need not we be afraid to lie in the grave?

When did Jesus rise again?

XLIV.

Who came early to the grave?

What did Mary see?

What was Mary afraid had happened ?
What two men came to the grave ?
Who got there first ?
Who went in first ?
What did they see ?
What did Mary see ?
What did Mary say to the stranger ?
How did she find out who He was ?
Who saw Jesus first after He had risen ?

XLV.

When did three women come to the garden ?
What surprised them very much ?
What did they find in the tomb ?
What did the angel promise them ?
Whom did they meet ?
What did Jesus say to them ?

XLVI.

How did Jesus surprise the disciples ?
What did He say to them ?
How did they know it was really Jesus who
spoke to them ?

What did He do to make them see He was really alive again ?

XLVII.

To what mountain did Jesus go with His disciples ?

What happened on the mountain ?

Who comforted the disciples ?

What did the angels promise them ?

Whom did Jesus send them ?

Who will be glad to see Jesus when He comes again ?

XLVIII.

What is the best news in the world ?

Who is the Holy Spirit ?

What did the Father do for the world ?

What did the Son do ?

What does the Holy Spirit do ?

What wonderful thing did the Holy Spirit make the disciples do ?

What did some wicked men say about this ?

Who preached the first sermon after Jesus went to Heaven ?

How many people repented ?

XLIX.

Who is the father of lies?
What lie did Ananias and Sapphira tell?
Why did they tell it?
What happened to Ananias?
How soon did Sapphira die too?
Where will liars go?

L.

Where did the angel tell Philip to go?
Whom did Philip see there?
What was the man in the chariot reading?
What question did the rich man ask Philip?
How did Philip answer him?
What did Philip do to the rich man?
How did the rich man feel as he returned
his own country?

Ll.

Why did Saul go to Damascus?
What happened on the way?
What did the Lord tell him to do?

Who came to Saul?

How did Saul spend the rest of his life?

What is Saul called now?

LII.

How did John show his love to Jesus?

How did Jesus show His love to John?

What did John see done to Jesus' dead body on the cross?

Where did John go when he was old?

What did he hear there?

What wonderful things did John see?

To whom will Jesus open the gates of Heaven?

Will Jesus come again to this world?

Works by the same Author

THE PEEP OF DAY;

OR

A Series of the EARLIEST RELIGIOUS INSTRUCTION the INFANT MIND is Capable of Receiving.

In a large type and with Eleven full-page Illustrations,
Printed in Colours by Marcus Ward. Imp. 16mo. cloth, 2s. 6d.

Also, 18mo. 27 Illust. cloth, 2s. ; roxburghe, gilt edges, 2s. 6d.
Cheap School Edition, limp cloth, with 27 Illustrations, 1s. 2d.
Popular Edition, limp cloth, with 24 Illustrations, 6d.

OVER 700,000 copies of this Book (published originally in 1833) have been sold in England at 2s. and 1s. 2d. There have been editions printed and sold by thousands in America ; and the work has been translated and published in French, German, Russian, Samoan, Chinese, and many other languages, both for Missionary and general Educational use.

The Indian Government, in their Educational Report for April, 1873, specially recommended the Work for use in their Mission-schools ; and Missionaries have testified to the fact that by having the book in English, and translating it verbatim, they have been enabled to bring the truths of the Bible within the comprehension and home to the hearts of the heathen when their own explanations have failed.

THE PEEP OF DAY:

A SERIES OF THE EARLIEST RELIGIOUS INSTRUCTION.

760th Thousand. 27 Illust. 18mo. cloth, 2s. ; roxburghe, 2s. d.
Authorized French Edition, Illustrated, no Questions, 2s. 6d.

STREAKS OF LIGHT;

Or, FIFTY-TWO FACTS FROM THE BIBLE.

70th Thousand. 52 Illust. 18mo. cloth, 2s. 6d. ; roxb. 3s.

LINE UPON LINE:

A SECOND SERIES OF RELIGIOUS INSTRUCTION.

Part I. 368th Thous. 30 Illust. 18mo. cloth, 2s. 6d. ; roxb. 3s.
Part II. 299th Thous. 27 Illust. 18mo. cloth, 2s. 6d. ; roxb. 3s.

PRECEPT UPON PRECEPT.

66th Thous. 68 Illust. and Map. 18mo. cloth, 2s. 6d. ; roxb. 3s.

APOSTLES PREACHING to Jews & Gentiles;

Or, THE ACTS EXPLAINED TO CHILDREN.

26th Thous. 27 Illustrations and Col. Map, cloth, 2s. 6d. ; roxb. 3s.

LINES LEFT OUT.

66th Thousand. 28 Illust. 18mo. cloth, 2s. 6d. ; roxb. 3s.

THE KINGS OF ISRAEL AND JUDAH.

31st Thousand. 27 Illust. and Col. Map, cloth, 2s. 6d. ; roxb. 3s.

THE CAPTIVITY OF JUDAH.

13th Thous. 27 Illust. and Col. Map. 18mo. cloth, 2s. 6d. ; roxb. 3s.

MORE ABOUT JESUS.

73rd Thousand. 26 Illust. 18mo. cloth, 2s. 6d. ; roxb. 3s.

Works by the same Author.

READING WITHOUT TEARS;

Or, A PLEASANT MODE OF LEARNING TO READ.

Part I. 76th Thousand. Sq. 16mo. 520 Illust. *large type*, 2s. 6d.
Part II. 33rd Thousand. Sq. 16mo. 130 Illust. *large type*, 2s. 6d.
(*Two Parts in One, cloth antique*, 4s. 6d.)

READING DISENTANGLED.

A Series of Classified Lessons, in 37 Sheets. 21st Edition.
Plain, 4s. the set; Mounted for hanging, 7s.
Coloured and Mounted, 10s.

THE ANGEL'S MESSAGE;

Or, THE SAVIOUR MADE KNOWN TO THE COTTAGER.

27th Thousand. **Square 16mo.** 9 Illustrations, paper cover, 2d.

LIGHT IN THE DWELLING;

Or, A HARMONY OF THE FOUR GOSPELS.

With short & simple Remarks adapted to Reading at Family Prayers
and arranged in 365 Sections for every day of the year.
30th Thousand. Thick 8vo. cloth, 6s.

THE NIGHT OF TOIL;

Or, AN ACCOUNT OF THE LABOURS OF THE
FIRST FOUR MISSIONARIES IN THE SOUTH-SEA ISLANDS.

7th and Cheaper Edition.
Fcap. 8vo. with 9 Illustrations and Coloured Map, cloth, 3s

CHEAP SCHOOL EDITIONS.

18mo. limp, with 340 Illustrations and 7 Maps.

THE PEEP OF DAY ... ... 1s. 2d.

STREAKS OF LIGHT ... ... 1s. 6d.

LINE UPON LINE. Two Parts, each 1s. 4d.

PRECEPT UPON PRECEPT ... ... 1s. 6d.

APOSTLES PREACHING ... ... 1s. 4d.

LINES LEFT OUT ... ... 1s. 6d.

KINGS OF ISRAEL AND JUDAH ... 1s. 6d.

CAPTIVITY OF JUDAH ... ... 1s. 6d.

MORE ABOUT JESUS ... ... 1s. 4d.

The First Volume is for 4, the last for 12 Years of Age.

THE PEEP OF DAY.

CHEAP POPULAR EDITION. 18mo. cloth, Illustrated, 6d.

LINE UPON LINE. 2 Vols.

CHEAP POPULAR EDITION. 18mo. cloth, Illustrated, each 9d.

Over 2,000,000 Copies of this Author's 22 Works have been sold.

HATCHARDS, PICCADILLY, LONDON.

GEOGRAPHIES FOR CHILDREN.

New Edition.   97th Thousand.   Carefully Revised.
NEAR HOME;
¡Or, THE COUNTRIES OF EUROPE DESCRIBED.

With Anecdotes.

With 22 full-page and 79 small Illustrations (50 perfectly new)
and Coloured Map.   **Crown** 8vo. cloth, 5*s*.

New Edition.   54th Thousand.   Carefully Revised.
FAR OFF (Part I.);
Or, ASIA DESCRIBED.   With Anecdotes.

With 16 full-page, 95 small, and 2 Coloured Illustrations,
and Coloured Map.   Crown 8vo. 5*s*.

New Edition.   39th Thousand.   Revised.
FAR OFF (Part II.);
Or, OCEANIA, AFRICA, AND AMERICA DESCRIBED.

With over 200 Illustrations and 2 Coloured Maps.
Crown 8vo. 5*s*.

HATCHARDS, PICCADILLY, LONDON.

A Handsome Presentation Box for the Young.

With 340 Illustrations and 7 Maps.

THE PEEP OF DAY SERIES.

BEST EDITION.   Ten 18mo. Vols. roxb. gilt edges, in box, 31s. 6d
CHEAP SCHOOL EDITION.   Ten vols. leatherette, in box, 21s.

CONTENTS.

THE PEEP OF DAY.

STREAKS OF LIGHT.

LINE UPON LINE.   Two Vols.

PRECEPT UPON PRECEPT.

APOSTLES PREACHING.

LINES LEFT OUT.

KINGS OF ISRAEL AND JUDAH.

CAPTIVITY OF JUDAH.

MORE ABOUT JESUS.

The First Volume is for 4, *the last for* 12 *Years of Age.*

HATCHARDS, PICCADILLY, LONDON.

www.ingramcontent.com/pod-product-compliance
Lightning Source LLC
Chambersburg PA
CBHW031350290326
41932CB00044B/856